T0108264

Making Marriage

Making Marriage

*Husbands, Wives, and the American State in
Dakota and Ojibwe Country*

Catherine J. Denial

 Minnesota Historical
Society Press

©2013 by the Minnesota Historical Society. All rights reserved.
No part of this book may be used or reproduced in any manner whatsoever
without written permission except in the case of brief quotations embodied in
critical articles and reviews. For information, write to the Minnesota Historical
Society Press, 345 Kellogg Blvd. W., St. Paul, MN 55102-1906.

www.mhspress.org

The Minnesota Historical Society Press is a member of the
Association of American University Presses.

Manufactured in the United States of America

10 9 8 7 6 5 4 3 2 1

♾ The paper used in this publication meets the minimum
requirements of the American National Standard for Information Sciences—
Permanence for Printed Library Materials, ANSI Z39.48–1984.

International Standard Book Number
ISBN: 978-0-87351-906-9 (paper)
ISBN: 978-0-87351-907-6 (e-book)

Library of Congress Cataloging-in-Publication Data

Denial, Catherine J., 1971–
Making marriage : husbands, wives, and the American state in Dakota and
Ojibwe country / Catherine J. Denial.
pages cm.
Includes bibliographical references and index.
ISBN 978-0-87351-906-9 (pbk. : alk. paper) — ISBN 978-0-87351-907-6 (ebook)
1. Dakota Indians—Marriage customs and rites—Minnesota. 2. Ojibwa Indians—
Marriage customs and rites—Minnesota. 3. Métis—Marriage customs
and rites—Minnesota. 4. Marriage customs and rites—Minnesota—History.
5. Minnesota—Social life and customs. I. Title.
E99.D1 D395 2013
305.897'52430776—DC23
2013013014

Image credits: pages 2, 26, 82, 130: Minnesota Historical Society collections; page 54:
courtesy the W. Duncan and Nivin MacMillan Foundation; page 106: LaBathe
Photo Collection of Alice Robinson.

IN MEMORY OF
Louise McNamara

Contents

Making Marriage

In this 1852 photograph, Dakota tipis still outnumber frame houses, only one of which is barely visible, at right.

Introduction

WHEN THE FIRST significant numbers of Americans arrived in the region now called Minnesota, they did so armed with the belief that good government and an orderly household went hand in hand. The territorial, state, and federal governments of the United States were built upon a particular vision of civic responsibility—that men, as heads of households, entered civic life on behalf of their dependents: wives, children, servants, and slaves. The political system of the United States was predicated upon this vision, overwhelmingly reserving suffrage, jury service, elected office, membership before the bar, and judicial appointments to white male heads of household and limiting the legal rights of all others by their degree of separation from that ideal. Women, children, servants, and slaves were legal dependents, owing labor and obedience to their husbands, fathers, and masters. Legal reality created cultural presumption (and vice versa): in myriad ways, dependents were publicly identified as unfit to make personal decisions or to involve themselves in business and government.[1]

These ideas clashed forcibly with the conceptions of kinship and social order that existed among the Upper Midwest's long-established Dakota, Ojibwe, and mixed-heritage communities. None of these communities readily acquiesced to the vision of family or government that Americans imported, and in their resistance to the gender and familial roles advocated by military personnel, Indian agents, and missionaries, the Native and mixed-heritage inhabitants of the Upper Midwest frustrated American attempts to transform Indian country into a state. Indeed, rather than gaining swift ascendancy in the region, many Americans were forced to compromise their own beliefs about marriage, divorce, and political propriety in order to create circumstances in which they could put down roots.

As politicians and men of power in the settled East debated territorial expansion, slavery, the meaning of *nation*, and the limits of Native sovereignty throughout the early nineteenth century, the inhabitants of the region that would one day become Minnesota tussled over the same questions in their interpersonal relationships. Daily trade logs, the professional and personal correspondence of area missionaries, records of government agents and military personnel, documents from regional clerks of court, and the personal records of settlers all illuminate the political nature of marriage in a region wrestling with change. Marriages of all kinds, and the households that marriages created, were inextricably bound up with questions of nation and identity for the Dakota, the Ojibwe, mixed-heritage individuals, and Americans alike. Through the stories of married— and divorcing—men and women in the region, we can trace the uneven fortunes of American expansion in the early nineteenth century and the nation-shaping power of marital acts.

The story of marriage and nation produced in the early nineteenth-century Upper Midwest had many beginnings. One was the American Revolution, and the philosophies of government that structured both independence and what came after. Another was woven into the policies the new United States adopted toward Indian nations. More were rooted in the Upper Midwest itself—in the landscape and natural resources of that particular place, and in Ojibwe and Dakota conceptions of government, kinship, and family. Each is important for our understanding of what took place in the region after 1819 and the ways in which imperialism and resistance were expressed through the bodies of husbands and wives.

"Do not put such unlimited power into the hands of the Husbands"

On March 31, 1776, Abigail Adams set aside her numerous responsibilities—four children to raise; illnesses to weather; soap to manufacture; cloth to spin; a spring planting to design; livestock to tend—and wrote to her absent husband, John, in Philadelphia. Abigail touched upon the business of their household but wrote mostly of political concerns. She asked for news of patriot defenses in Virginia, wondered whether men who kept others enslaved could ever truly value freedom, and urged her husband, a delegate to the Continental Congress, to "Remember the Ladies" in "the new Code of Laws which I suppose it will be necessary for you to make":

> Do not put such unlimited power into the hands of the Husbands. Remember all Men would be tyrants if they could. That your Sex are Naturally Tyrannical is a Truth so thoroughly established as to admit of no dispute . . . Why then, not put it out of the power of the

vicious and the Lawless to use us with cruelty and indignity with
impunity. Men of Sense in all Ages abhor those customs which treat
us only as the vassals of your Sex.[2]

Abigail's words were a critique of coverture, the system of laws in
each North American British colony that governed a woman's legal
status after marriage. Under Anglo common law, a single woman
surrendered the greater portion of her legal capabilities to her husband when she became a wife. Trusts, premarital agreements, the
discretion of courts holding equity jurisdiction, and criminal acts
could all create exceptions to this general rule, but a woman was typ-
ically considered to be under the legal "wing, protection, and cover"
of her husband during marriage. A husband controlled his wife's
property, any income she earned, her ability to sue, sexual access to
her body, and her ability to contract. There was little legal protection
for a woman whose husband beat her, drank in excess, or failed to
adequately provide for his family. Divorce was hard to come by—
in Abigail's Massachusetts, for example, only forty-six petitions for
divorce came before the General Court between 1765 and 1774, and
of these, just twenty-four were approved.[3]

John Adams's reply, penned on April 14, was unequivocal: "We
know better than to repeal our masculine systems," he wrote. While
Abigail's aims in raising the subject of marital law with John may have
been modest—biographer Edith Gelles suggests that Abigail so valued her position as wife and mother that she asked for protections
so that women might better perform those tasks, not immeasurably
alter them—John was concerned with the larger implications of her
plea. "We have been told that our Struggle has loosened the bands
of Government every where. That Children and Apprentices were

disobedient—that schools and Colleges were grown turbulent—that Indians slighted their Guardians and Negroes grew insolent to their Masters," he wrote. The rhetoric of liberty, most recently fanned by the publication of Thomas Paine's *Common Sense* (a treatise John sent to Abigail in February), seemed to threaten every structure of power that had given cohesion to colonial life before the Revolutionary War. Mindful of this, John not only refused Abigail's suggestion that marital law should be altered but downplayed its importance, suggesting the power of husbands over wives was "little more than Theory. We dare not exert our Power in its full Latitude. We are obliged to go fair, and softly, and in Practice you know We are the subjects." Nevertheless, he hoped that "General Washington, and all our brave Heroes would fight" rather than see any alteration to coverture that would "subject Us to the Despotism of the Peticoat [*sic*]."[4]

That John and Abigail's disagreement was meant to be a private affair—neither could reasonably have imagined the attention historians would later lavish upon these letters—does not lessen its power as a demonstration of the consanguinity of married and civic life. In practical terms, the dispute between the colonies and Great Britain impinged upon Abigail's ability to perform the services of a wife. Her husband was called away—she both missed him and worried about raising her children without "the example of a Father constantly before them." Her Boston townhouse was, for a time, occupied by the British, and her Braintree home shook with the "roar of Cannon" throughout the spring of 1776. Basic provisions were hard to come by, necessitating increased labor within the household: "I find as much as I can do to manufacture cloathing [*sic*] for my family which would else be Naked," Abigail wrote to John. Even after the British quit Boston, she wrote, "As to goods of any kind, we cannot tell what quantity there is. Only two or three Shops [were] open. Goods at a most extravagant price." John, for his part, regretted that he could not be of greater assistance to her, offered suggestions for the proper education of their children, and lamented, "Instead of domestic Felicity, I am destined to public Contentions . . . In the Place of private Peace, I must be distracted with the . . . Vexation of developing the deep Intrigues of Politicians and must assist in conducting the arduous Operations of War." Both made private sacrifices in order to see the colonies succeed in matters of military, economic, and political import. "Retirement, Rural quiet, Domestick pleasure, all must give place to the weighty cares of State," wrote Abigail. "[I] think myself, well rewarded, if my private Pleasure and Interest are sacrificed as they ever have been and will be, to the Happiness of others," wrote John.[5]

Marriage and civic responsibility were intertwined not only practically but also philosophically. The American Revolution drew on the intellectual traditions of the Enlightenment, particularly the theories of social contract advanced by men such as Thomas Hobbes, John Locke, and Jean-Jacques Rousseau. Each argued that a just government depended upon the consent of the governed—that man was born into unfettered liberty but in time found it prudent to surrender this unlimited freedom in exchange for the mutual protection of life and property that might be achieved by a fraternity of citizens. Such was the social contract, an agreement for all men to be equally bound by law and to defend a community's sovereignty. Hobbes, Locke, and Rousseau disagreed about the best manner in which this government might be practically realized—could monarchy persist within such a framework?—but each agreed that consent was intrinsic to any semblance of just rule. They also agreed that only men could enter into the contract, the subjection of women to men—perfected in the marriage contract—precluding them from participating in civil life. The reasons for this were only superficially addressed. Locke suggested that woman's subjection to man had been the order of the universe since Eve was made from Adam's rib; in his *Social Contract*, Rousseau passed no comment at all.[6]

But as political philosopher Carole Pateman has argued, the forcible subjection of woman to man was implied within the logical structures of the theories each philosopher proposed. Hobbes, Locke, and Rousseau agreed that the family was the first form of human association—it predated civil society and occurred in the state of nature. Yet if, in theory, humans in this state lived by reference to what would best secure their "Self-preservation ... [their] chief and almost sole concern" being the exercise of "those faculties that are most concerned with attack or defence, either for overcoming his prey, or for preventing him from becoming the prey of other animals," it followed that no woman would voluntarily become pregnant and no families could exist. Pregnancy would slow a woman's movement and increase the amount of sustenance she required to survive—in the "nasty, brutish" world described by Hobbes, Locke, and Rousseau, it would constitute an illogical handicap. Family therefore had to be established upon the forcible subjection of women—upon men compelling women to become pregnant, bear children, and accept the protection of a husband-become-father rather than protecting themselves. This excluded women from the pool of those who might enter into the social contract, as they no longer had untrammeled liberty to exchange for the protection of law. Men became woman's civil representative—the subjection of women was rendered natural, their exclusion from civic matters innate.[7]

Thus, when Thomas Paine wrote in *Common Sense* that Americans were owed a "government of our own . . . a constitution of our own," his actors were—by the customs, philosophies, and lived experiences of the era—not universal figures, but men with responsibilities to a household. Political virtue and family life were inseparable; the performance of one set of duties required the performance of the other, and failure as a patriot and failure as a husband were linked. Those who believed that the English system of government was just, for example, were, to Paine, like men "attached to a prostitute . . . unfitted to choose or judge of a wife." Further, the British government had outright targeted the American household for destruction. "Hath your house been burnt? Hath your property been destroyed before your face? Are your wife and children destitute of a bed to lie on, or bread to live on?" Paine asked his readers. Any man who had endured these acts and still advocated for peace with the British was, Paine argued, "unworthy [of] the name of husband, father, friend, or lover, and whatever may be your rank or title in life, you have the heart of a coward, and the spirit of a sycophant."[8]

These matters took on a practical bent with the coming of independence. On May 10, 1776, the Continental Congress resolved that the colonies should "adopt such government as shall, in the opinion of the representatives of the people, best conduce to the happiness and safety of their constituents in particular, and America in general." One by one, the colonies, then the states, debated who should participate in government and enshrined their decisions in law. The work took five years to complete; it took five years, likewise, for the Articles of Confederation, which offered structure to the new national government, to be ratified. The states created constitutions as varied as their local cultures, environments, economies, and systems of labor. Vermont extended suffrage to all free adult men; Pennsylvania's lawmakers extended the vote to any man who paid taxes; Virginia retained existing property qualifications for suffrage; Massachusetts made property ownership a requisite for voting where no property qualifications had existed before. Some states created unicameral legislatures, others preferred upper and lower houses, and there were experiments with term limits written into several of the constitutions. Free black men who met the stated property requirements for suffrage in New Hampshire could vote; free black men in South Carolina could not. No agreement existed between the colonies on what government should be except on the matter of a participant's gender. In every state, men owed militia service in defense of their country. In almost every state voters were male.[9]

Only New Jersey allowed women to vote. The innovation was significant in that it demonstrated women were not constitutionally unsuited to participate in electoral government—the fabric of New Jersey society was not pulled apart by this new female responsibility, nor were female voters made masculine by the act (fears voiced both at the time and for many years to come). Yet the expansion of suffrage to women in New Jersey had little impact elsewhere—no other state or territory extended suffrage to women until 1869, and New Jersey itself rescinded female suffrage in 1808. More significant than what New Jersey changed is what New Jersey and every other state did not. Coverture survived the Revolution; women were, by the dictates of custom, religion, and economics, expected to marry, and once married, their legal status was subsumed beneath that of their husbands. The brief expansion of New Jersey suffrage to women was necessarily limited, as suffrage was granted only to female property owners, and since no married woman could own property, no married woman could vote. By law, all but widows and adult single women were marked as dependent; by custom and economics, all but the wealthiest spinsters and widows needed to wed. Combined, these facts made women the very antithesis of the citizen that male Revolutionaries valued. Self-sufficiency, self-reliance, independence—these were the hallmarks of republican citizenship, and all were coded as male.[10]

The Constitution of the United States—penned and ratified after the Revolutionary War was won and peace was revealed to be a messy, expensive, regionally partisan experience—explicitly framed the responsibilities and obligations of government in terms of the social contract. "We the People"—the men of the former colonies—surrendered their unfettered liberty for "a more perfect Union" that would "insure domestic Tranquility, provide for the common defense, promote the general Welfare," and, in language that linked civic and household responsibilities, "secure the Blessings of Liberty to ourselves and our Posterity." Women were (as in Hobbes's, Locke's, and Rousseau's philosophies) implicitly but never explicitly acknowledged, the reproductive work of their bodies necessary in order for "our Posterity" to exist, their political wants subsumed and assumed by independent men. Coverture was affirmed as a foundational principle of the Republic, an intrinsic part of good government, ordering the proper political roles of women as well as men.[11]

The interdependence of orderly households and good government became particularly important to the thinking of those men who directed American Indian policy in the early Republic. Throughout the 1780s, Americans along the fringes of settled country demonstrated a dedication to pushing farther west, frequently antagonizing those American Indian nations to whom the land they coveted belonged. Faced with an insufficient treasury and a national distaste for prolonged military engagement, numerous members of government concluded that the only way to manage such border skirmishes—if not all-out war—was to implement a program of "civilizing" American Indian people. "The disposition of the people of the States to emigrate into the Indian country cannot be effectually prevented," wrote Secretary of War Henry Knox to President George Washington in 1789. "It may be restrained by postponing new purchasses [*sic*] of Indian territory, and by prohibiting the Citizens from intruding on the Indian Lands. It may be regulated by forming Colonies under the direction of Government and by posting a body of troops to execute their orders . . . [but] How different would be the sensation of a philosophic mind to reflect that instead of exterminating a part of the human race by our modes of population that we had persevered through all difficulties and at last had imparted our Knowledge of cultivation, and the arts, to the Aboriginals of the Country."[12]

Knox allowed that a program of "civilization" would take time to establish but considered it the most prudent policy the federal government could adopt and offered a detailed vision of its implementation. "Were it possible to introduce among the Indian tribes a love for exclusive property it would be a happy commencement of the business," he began. "This might be brought about by making presents from time to time to the Chiefs or their Wives of sheep and other domestic animals . . . [plus] persons . . . appointed to take charge and teach the use of them." This bucolic state would be aided and abetted by Christian preaching. "Missionaries of excellent moral character should be appointed to reside in their nation," Knox wrote, "who should be well supplied with all the implements of husbandry and the necessary stock for a farm."[13]

All of these principles played out in the federal laws related to Indian communities between 1790 and 1819. The 1793 Trade and Intercourse Act stated that, "in order to promote civilization among the friendly Indian tribes . . . [they will] be furnished with useful domestic animals, and implements of husbandry . . . [The president shall] appoint such persons, from time to time, as temporary agents, to reside among the Indians, as he shall think proper." That year, Congress allocated an initial sum of $20,000 for this program, plus another $50,000 in 1795; in 1796 the sum was set at $15,000 per year. Specific treaties offered further detail. Article 12 of the 1790 treaty between the Creek nation and the United States articulated the American hope "That the Creek nation may be led to a greater degree of civilization, and . . . become herdsmen and cultivators, instead of remaining in a state of hunters." To that end, the United States promised to "furnish gratuitously . . . useful domestic animals and implements of husbandry." Similar articles were written into treaties with the Cherokee in 1791, the Iroquois confederacy in 1794, the Wyandot, Delaware, Shawanese, Ottawa, Miamis, and Ojibwe in 1795, and the Kaskaskia in 1803. An 1804 treaty between the Delaware and the United States was particularly direct in describing the connection between agricultural gifts and federal policy. The Delaware were promised three hundred dollars a year for ten years for "the purpose of ameliorating their condition and promoting their civilization," in support of which the United States would find "suitable persons" to teach the Delaware "to make fences, cultivate the earth, and [learn] such of the domestic arts as are adapted to their situation." In 1805, the Cherokee were promised "useful articles of, and machines for, agriculture," while the Creeks, the Ottawa, and the Osage were promised blacksmiths "to mend their arms and utensils of husbandry" in 1805, 1807, and 1808.[14]

At issue was nothing less than the remaking of American Indian households. As Nancy Cott has argued, in most American Indian communities with whom the U.S. government was negotiating, "men hunted and the women were the agriculturalists, making their sexual division of labor dramatically different from what white Americans expected and associated with gender propriety—men working the fields and women caring for the house." Travelers, essayists, and politicians interpreted women's agricultural and domestic labor as drudgery and expressed scorn for the idea that hunting was appropriate male work. American Indian households seemed dangerously disordered. In many communities, men and women could separate as easily as they had married, while children might trace their lineage through the female line. Some communities permitted polygamy; few communities had any notion of property that matched that of non-Native observers. In a nation that had made coverture foundational to the organization of government and civic life, American Indian systems of kinship were insupportable. Providing agents, instruction, tools, and animals with the goal of urging men into the fields and women into the home was, as much as the accumulation of land by purchase and treaty agreement, a tool by which the United States hoped to transform Indian land into American territory.[15]

An 1817 treaty with the Cherokee made the link between "civilization" and coverture explicit. In article 8 of that treaty, the U.S. government offered "each and every head of any Indian family . . . who may wish to become citizens of the United States," 640 acres of land for life, "with a reversion in fee simple to their children" after death. This inheritance, however, reserved "to the widow her dower," a mechanism in Anglo-American law that gave widows the use of one-third of their late husband's property, real and personal, until they died or married again. Dower rights sprang from a recognition of the dependency of wives—that few widows had the financial means to avoid becoming a burden on the state—and extended a husband's provision for her needs even after his death. Dower was not a Cherokee value but a component of the U.S. government's commitment to reorganizing American Indian gender roles, marital responsibilities, and concepts of property ownership.[16]

These, then, were the beliefs about government, marriage, and family that Americans carried with them into the Upper Midwest and which conditioned their actions, perspective, and understanding of the region. "And must this healthy, fertile country always lie waste; unsettled, uncultivated, and uninhabited only by wild beasts and men as ignorant and wild as they?" asked missionary Jedediah Stevens as he entered the region for the first time in 1829. "May we not hope & believe that this desert where nothing is now heard but the hooting of the savages, the firing of his gun & the yells of wild beasts . . . will ere long become a fruitful cultivated field: . . . [that instead of] the comfortless shelter of barks which they carry in their canoes and upon their backs, will be seen comfortable dwelling house & barns, filled with a plenty for man & beast[?]"[17]

BEFORE ALL OTHER THINGS

Yet this is not the whole story; the tale of those philosophies, ideas, and policies that were rooted on the eastern seaboard provides only partial context for the interactions that took place in the Upper Midwest after 1819. The region was not merely another Massachusetts, another Maryland, another South Carolina—it was its own place and had its own inhabitants and its own stories already at work.[18]

The Upper Midwest was prairie country, threaded through by rivers and peppered with lakes, scorched in summer and bitterly cold

in the winter months. Ash, oak, linden, and birch grew by the waterways, wild rice at the lakes, and each spring the maples filled with rising sap. There were violets, wild roses, and vast rolling oceans of
prairie grass. Ducks, plover, fish, and turtles; muskrat, beaver, otter,
and deer; bears, buffalo, elk, and mosquitoes flourished season by season. The Dakota and Ojibwe managed the resources that surrounded
them, burning the prairies, planting corn, hunting and fishing over
vast distances, and gathering wild turnips, berries, and acorns. Reeds
and rushes became mats; birch bark and hides were stretched and
woven into shelters; trees were transformed into canoes.[19]

For the Ojibwe, the Upper Midwest was the end point of their
spiritual and physical journey from the eastern seaboard, the place
from which their modern community had grown and spread. Ojibwe
oral tradition preserves the memory of that migration as a slow
movement of people from "the great salt water" of the Atlantic along
the St. Lawrence River to Lake Huron and then to the eastern edge
of Lake Superior near Sault Ste. Marie. It was on those shores that
the Ojibwe made their home, with Madeline Island, La Pointe, and
Fond du Lac all figuring large in migration memory. The La Pointe
Ojibwe consider the western shores of Lake Superior "the root from
which all the far scattered villages of the tribe have sprung," the place,
added nineteenth-century observer William Warren, "from which
the Ojibway band first grew, and like a tree it has spread branches
in every direction." The birch-bark scrolls of the Midewiwin society at
Leech Lake memorialize this migration and dispersal in pictograph
form, while seventeenth-century French fur trade documents captured the same process in letters, memoirs, and maps identifying
the "Outchibouec," "Outchibous," and "Outchipoue" as of particular note among the disparate, autonomous Algonquin bands of the
Upper Great Lakes.[20]

This, then, was a temporal history—but the Ojibwe understanding of place also draws from non-temporal stories explaining the creation of the world and the responsibility of the people—the Anishinaabe—to that world. Kitchi-Manitou, the creator, existed before all other things; it was at Kitchi-Manitou's behest that Muzzu-Kummik-Quae (Mother Earth) was created, as well as all animal and plant life, the manitous of air and water, and the people who existed in relationship to it all. It was from Kitchi-Manitou's emissary, Nanabush, that the Ojibwe learned how to care for the world, to live within expansive kinship systems of responsibility and reciprocity that took deliberate intention and commitment to maintain. Lakes, hills, rock, thunder, lightning, wind, birds, fish, and more—all had the power to bless, to teach, and to hinder the activities of communities and individuals. To be Ojibwe in the early nineteenth century was to live as a distinct community in a tangible place with tangible resources—but also to recognize and respect the intangible networks of power that existed within, beyond, and before rock, river, tree, and child.[21]

Ojibwe social organization and governance were rooted in this understanding of place. The primary units of social organization were clans, best understood as large family groups. In temporal terms, the first clans derived their identities from the Algonquin communities who had named themselves in relation to the bird or animal life that surrounded them in the Upper Great Lakes, including Crane, Loon, Bear, Catfish, Moose, and Marten. In Ojibwe stories of migration, however, the temporal and the non-temporal merge. As one nineteenth-century elder remembered it, Crane had "circled slowly above the Great Fresh Water Lakes . . . looking for a resting place, till it lit on a hill overlooking Boweting (Sault Ste.

Marie) . . . and chose its first resting place," calling others to join it and establishing the Ojibwe nation. These clans—and those that were added in successive years by Ojibwe establishing villages further from Lake Superior—were, in the words of French explorer Joseph Nicollet, "an institution of a purely civic nature," a family identity that determined whom an individual could and could not marry and to whom they had obligations of deference and support. By the nineteenth century, many Ojibwe village sites were home to two or three clans, with allied family groups coming together in larger numbers to trade or make war. Out of these clans rose leaders as time and circumstance demanded. No single leader dominated any family group; orators, diplomats, and those skilled in warfare came forward as their skills were needed and stepped down when their work was done. Leadership was not hereditary; it lasted only as long as a man could effectively meet the needs his larger family faced, which in turn reconnected governance to place. Defending territory against outsiders, deciding the most judicious use of the region's natural resources, determining when and where to hunt—these were among a leader's responsibilities.[22]

Unlike the Ojibwe, the Dakota claim no migratory history—the Upper Midwest has always been their home. The region had once been the territory of the entire Dakota confederacy, including the Teton and Yankton who had, by the nineteenth century, expanded into the western plains. The borders of upper midwestern Dakota country, however, shifted only after the arrival of the Ojibwe to the north prompted competition for land and natural resources between the two groups. The names by which the Dakota describe their world speak to their long tenure in the region, the natural resources that support their way of life, and moments of crisis that individuals and communities had survived. In 1838 Joseph Nicollet recorded that "on the left bank [of the Credit River] enters the little stream . . . where they killed the woman = *Winodshirteha Ktepi watpadan.* This Sioux woman, whom the Chippewa believed they had left dead after scalping her, lived, and one of her daughters who is now very old has grandchildren, who have grandchildren"—a story that captures the connection of six generations of Dakota to one place. Nicollet also visited "*Oksida nom Witcha Ktepi*—the place where the young men were killed (by the Sauk)," a marsh just a short distance from "*kanrhanzi witcha ktepi* . . . the river where the Kansas were killed," as well as Tchan Shasha Yankedan (where there is redwood), Watpa ipakshan (the river which bends), and Mderhabetichi (lake where the pelicans make their nests). There was Watopapidan (the lake where they go in canoes), iyansha K'api (the place where one digs the red rock), and Titanka hé (the place of the great lodge), where summer camps were established during the hunt. All these names and associated stories speak to the Dakota's deep connection to place.[23]

The Dakota's temporal history in the Upper Midwest existed alongside and within a history of events and powers that were outside time. In 1913, Dakota scholar Amos Oneroad retold the story of the world's origins in the mud that Muskrat retrieved from beneath the weight of the ocean—mud that a female Unktehi (water monster) helped transform into the physical body of the earth. Contemporary Dakota historian Waziyatawin roots her critique of Minnesota land policy in stories that memorialize the creation of the Dakota from the very core of Ina Maka (Mother Earth) at Bdote (present-day Mendota, where the Mississippi and Minnesota rivers meet). In these remembrances of origin, as in countless stories of the interaction between spirits, animals, birds, and humans, the Dakota capture their responsibility to the world in which they live, to their ancestors, to the people yet to come, and to the spiritual powers—some mischievous, some caring, some sly, some benevolent—with which they interact in their myriad forms. "Dakota worldview recognizes a spiritual essence in all creation," Waziyatawin writes, "and much time and energy is [and was] dedicated to developing positive interactions with these spiritual beings." The Upper Midwest is the site of the Dakota people's beginning, a place that gave shape to their original bodies and to which they owe their continued life.[24]

The primary unit of social organization among the nineteenth-century Dakota was the family. Most immediately, this meant the *tiyospaye,* the extended network of family with whom individuals interacted on a daily basis, but in more general terms, it encompassed the entire Dakota nation. Kinship enabled the Dakota to distinguish friends from enemies; someone who joined a camp circle but who could not establish a kinship connection to those already there was regarded with deep suspicion. An individual might be kin because of blood connection, marriage, or social adoption, and each form of kinship determined that individual's relationship to others, their responsibilities, their obligations, and the taboos of social interaction they must observe. Government was rooted in kinship. Leaders (always male and hereditary) might diffuse hostilities by calling on the parties to recognize their kinship responsibilities to each other; crimes were punished in light of the damage done to kinship ties; adoption of captives was one way to bring about peace after war. Grandparents, aunts, uncles, parents, husbands, wives, cousins, sons, and daughters were kin, but those terms were also extended to other inhabitants of the natural world and to spirits untethered by time. As Dakota scholar Ella Deloria summarized, "kinship relationship was the very texture of Dakota life; . . . it was not a detachable adjunct but, rather, its very heart . . . its all-pervading, all-enveloping essence."[25]

In time, European explorers, traders, and missionaries moved into these indigenous spaces, long before Americans arrived in the Upper Midwest. They brought other ways of understanding the world with them, particularly Catholicism, with its attendant conception of a world created by a single divinity that existed outside creation, not within it. Traders saw economic opportunity in the beaver, muskrat, deer, and buffalo that existed in subsistence, kinship, and ritual relationship to the Dakota and Ojibwe, and brought new goods to the interior—blankets, iron pots, sewing needles, guns. Yet it was incumbent upon these non-Native individuals to take up the kinship duties and responsibilities of the Dakota and Ojibwe if they wanted tenure in the Upper Midwest, be it by appeals to fictive relationships (son, brother, and father in the case of priests) or by marriage and parenthood (in the case of traders). Newcomers were expected to share resources, to be fair in their dealings with family members, and to show deference to elders if their endeavors—spiritual or mercantile—were to succeed. All parties were changed by these encounters, but this was Indian country, and Dakota and Ojibwe worldviews continued to persist.[26]

A SENSE OF PLACE

This, then, was the physical place, overwritten with multiple stories of origin and meaning, into which Colonel Henry Leavenworth led the Fifth Infantry in 1819. Sent to establish a fort as a first foothold for the United States in the region, Leavenworth carried with him the cultural and political beliefs of a well-born, married Yankee lawyer who had served as a soldier and a state legislator in recent years. He, and the military men, Indian agents, Protestant missionaries, American traders, and settlers who followed, came into contact with Dakota, Ojibwe, and mixed-heritage individuals who had their own fully developed ideas about kinship and government. In the clash between these systems of belief is the story of Minnesota's beginning—a complex, uneven tale, which does not offer a narrative of easy triumph for the American state.[27]

Chapter One of this book explores the story of Pelagie Faribault, the Dakota wife of a French trader, who gained ownership of Pike's Island at the junction of the Minnesota and Mississippi rivers in the Leavenworth-Dakota treaty of 1820. Faribault gained the island as a Dakota woman and maintained ownership over it for many years despite the attempts of several U.S. government officials to nullify her claim because she was married. To representatives of the U.S. government, Faribault should have been a woman who lived within the dictates of coverture—but she was not, and they could not mold her to be such, despite repeated attempts. In 1858, Faribault's family received $12,000 from the U.S. government in full recognition of her Dakota title and claim.

Chapter Two analyzes the meaning of marriage in the life of Mary Riggs, a missionary who journeyed from Massachusetts to the Upper Midwest in 1836 to make her life in Dakota country. Riggs was, with her husband, intent upon the conversion of the Dakota to Christianity, a feat she believed could be effected in no small part by the Dakota adopting marital practices identical to her own. She saw little success in this quest during her years at Lac qui Parle, as the Dakota were more than happy with the marital practices they already had and did not attach the same meaning to spinning, weaving, and knitting as Mary, who saw such tasks as foundational for a civilized life.

Mary did witness changes in the marital practices of traders, however—changes that foreshadowed the new demands that would be made of regional families by the American state.

For the officers at Fort Snelling, living a "civilized" life meant a wife, a household, and the domestic help that would preserve distinctions of rank and social currency between those inside the garrison and those without. Chapter Three explores the ways in which domestic activity was an act of public consequence at the garrison— the ways in which marriages produced "society" and "civilization" and the ways in which slavery was integral to the creation of both. The labor of slaves at the fort took place at some distance from mainstream American society, and this chapter explores the ways in which enslaved men and women had the opportunity to maintain relationships and households that would have been all but impossible elsewhere.

Chapter Four examines marriage in its breakdown through the 1840 divorce of Margaret McCoy, a part-Ojibwe woman, from her husband, Joseph Brown. Margaret and Joseph's divorce was granted to the parties by the Wisconsin territorial legislature "on account of the hostile incursions of Sioux Indians" against them. Such a decision defied social, legal, and cultural precedent in a region where American legislators were consciously trying to remake society into something more recognizable to themselves, and tells us how very far they had to go in this quest.

⁂

One morning, after a long dream in which he saw children, men, and women climb four hills, descending valleys between, losing many of their number along the way, Weegwauss (Birch) sought Chejauk's

(Crane's) wisdom. "It was a good dream, Weegwauss," said Crane. "You saw man's life in its entirety, in all its stages, in all its moods, and in all its forms. Kitchi-Manitou, the Great Spirit, has been generous to you." The dream, Crane interpreted, showed the hard work it took to reach old age and the losses—of children, of companions, of family, of friends—that accompanied that process. "While men and women contend with the struggles in the physical order, they must live out their visions," Crane counseled. "They must follow the path of life as is prescribed in the visions. In doing so they must observe the laws of the world and the customs of the community." Crane smoked as he talked, and he ended his interpretation by reflecting on all that he did not yet know. "I have given to you what I have understood," he said. "There is more, but my mind cannot compass the depth and scope of the thoughts of wise men on the subject of life. I leave it to you to grasp it in your own way, in your own time, and according to the powers of your mind and heart. Think on it."[28]

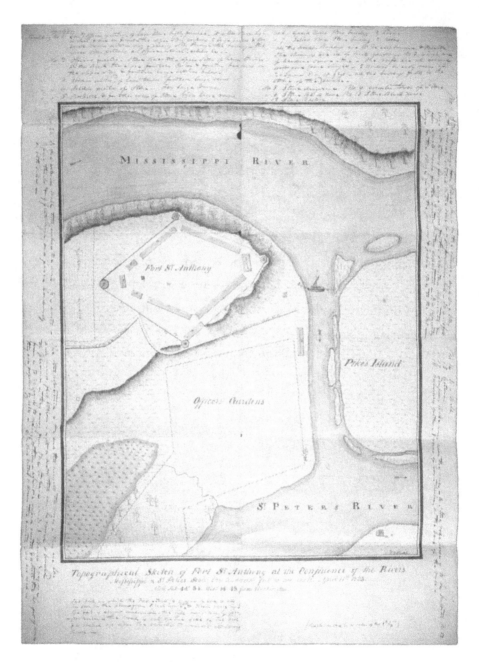

The close proximity of Pike's Island to Fort Snelling fueled wrangles over its ownership throughout the early nineteenth century.

CHAPTER ONE

Pelagie Faribault's Island

O N AUGUST 9, 1820, Colonel Henry Leavenworth welcomed interpreter Duncan Campbell, Indian agent Lawrence Talia-ferro, fur trader Jean Baptiste Faribault, and twenty-three local Dakota men to the place he called Camp Coldwater, the temporary home of the U.S. Fifth Infantry, just above the juncture of the St. Peter's (Minnesota) and Mississippi rivers. Leavenworth's goal was to finalize an agreement to construct a permanent fort in the Upper Midwest. By the day's end the assembled Dakota had signed a contract gifting a fifteen-acre reserve overlooking the rivers to the U.S. military, and within a month construction of Fort St. Anthony (renamed Fort Snelling in 1825) had begun.[1]

The contract signed by Leavenworth, six of his officers, Taliaferro, Faribault, and the Dakota leaders was short but precise. The Dakota, by signing the contract with their marks, were considered by Leaven-worth to "have given, granted, conveyed, and confirmed" title to a mil-itary reserve to the U.S. government. The boundaries of the acreage were described in reference to a number of markers—rivers, caves, the military's temporary encampment, and the villages in which Dakota leaders Little Crow, Black Dog, and White Bustard lived. Finally, the contract acknowledged two other land grants: a one-square-mile tract of land to Duncan Campbell, interpreter and kin to several local Dakota people; and ownership of Pike's Island in the middle of the Mississippi River to Pelagie Faribault, wife of trader Jean Baptiste and kin to Little Crow's band.[2]

A shallow reading of the treaty document tells us little about the region into which the United States had begun to expand or, crucially, the opinions of the people already living there about this intrusion. The document is dry, the prose sparse and bureaucratic. It provides a handful of certainties: that thirty-one men conducted business on this spot on that day. In the histories of the region that followed American settlement, the moment was preserved because it was seen as uncomplicated and pivotal: the United States had arrived; more Americans would follow; more edifices would be built. The treaty signaled the beginning of the end for established patterns of living among the region's Native and mixed-heritage inhabitants.

Yet Pelagie Faribault's presence in the document greatly complicates that story. If the 1820 treaty gave notice that the American state had its eyes set upon the Upper Midwest, it also indicated—through Pelagie—the strength of the cultural systems already in place in the region and the ability of Native and mixed-heritage individuals to frustrate the transformation of Indian country into an American state. In Euro-American law and custom, Pelagie should not have received land in her own right. But she did, and she not only received it but maintained ownership over it even as Euro-Americans became more populous in the region and insisted that a married woman of French and Indian ancestry should own nothing at all. In 1858, the

U.S. government paid Pelagie's heirs $12,000 for the land, even though Congress never ratified the 1820 treaty. It is through Pelagie's life, and the lives of other women like her, relegated to the fringes of the documentary record, that we discover a more complex story than many conventional histories allow.[3]

When Colonel Henry Leavenworth entered the Upper Midwest in 1819, he did so as a representative of a powerful, if fledgling, empire whose imperial designs he well understood. American settlement had by that year pushed through the Ohio country and into the regions that would become Michigan, Indiana, and Illinois. The United States was bent upon a program of westward expansion and looked to the Upper Midwest as the next step in expanding its influence into the northern prairies and plains. The establishment of military installations along the western edge of the Republic was a key step in this process, an act expressing the United States' belief in its own jurisdiction over the region and creating the means by which such jurisdiction might take practical form. Forts helped the United States direct westward development, with members of the military often charged with policing the transportation and sale of alcohol, settling disputes over trade, offering protection to missionaries and travelers, negotiating coexistence between Native groups and incoming settlers, and securing cooperation and land cessions from American Indian communities. Soldiers stationed at forts were also charged with the business of physically transforming the landscape—building defenses, clearing woods and prairie to make fields, and improving transportation and communication links to more populated areas.[4]

It was not the first time that Americans had entered this country, nor was the 1820 treaty the first brokered between the Dakota and the American state. Fifteen years before Leavenworth convened his treaty party at the Minnesota and Mississippi rivers, Dakota leaders, in negotiations with Lieutenant Zebulon Pike, ceded 100,000 acres of Dakota land to the U.S. government "for the purpose of the establishment of military posts." Pike had been immensely proud of the agreement, boasting to his commanding officer that "we have obtained about 100,00 Acres for a Song."[5]

Yet the fortunes of the ceded land were complex. Pike explored the Upper Mississippi in the name of a government that claimed jurisdiction there, but his journey took him into the heart of country replete with British, not American, influence. What inroads Pike was able to make for the American government during his trip into the region were quickly undermined by the United States' inability to fully support trade relationships with Native communities after the fact. Native political allegiances in the Midwest were inextricably bound up with economic partnerships and, with Americans offering few trade opportunities either as individuals or as representatives of the U.S. government, Native people paid the Republic little mind. Even after Americans blocked British trade vessels in their progress across the Great Lakes in 1807, effectively creating an embargo on British trade, the result was an increase in smuggling and general discord among Native groups rather than greater cooperation between Americans and Native communities in the Upper Midwest. The Americans made British trade difficult but did not insinuate themselves into the region as replacements, and thus there was little to encourage Native communities to ally themselves with the United States. This state of affairs persisted through the War of 1812.[6]

The effect of peace upon the fur trade was perhaps more important than the effect of war. The 1815 Treaty of Ghent, which outlined the terms of peace, did not change the political boundaries of the Upper Midwest in the ways Native people had wanted, nor which non-Native powers claimed jurisdiction in the region. British traders had fought for the opportunity to expand their economic sphere of influence; the Dakota had fought for the right to govern their own country without interference from Britain or the United States. The wishes of both parties were ignored, and the Dakota joined the Ojibwe in their long-standing resentment of the British trade system. While American traders were not yet, in 1815, positioned to take advantage of the fact, British traders found themselves on culturally and financially unstable ground. The ability of any individual trader or colonial power to satisfy the trade demands of Native groups remained centrally important to their consolidation of power.[7]

If Pike's 1805 agreement was complicated by economic reality, legal factors muddied the waters even more. President Thomas Jefferson had never officially sanctioned Pike's expedition into the Upper Midwest. General James Wilkinson of St. Louis unilaterally ordered Pike into the region instead (likely as a means to advance his own political career), and while the expedition met Jefferson's subsequent approval, it did not carry the president's blessing or absorb his attention in the same manner as the concurrent travels of Lewis and Clark. Jefferson was consequently lackadaisical in forwarding the 1805 treaty Pike negotiated with the Dakota to the Senate. Transmitted to Congress in 1808, the treaty was ratified but never proclaimed to be in effect by the president. The treaty was therefore moot within the dictates of Euro-American law.[8]

Ratification and proclamation of the treaty proved, to some extent, beside the point for all parties concerned. Treaties were not a Euro-American invention—agreements between Native communities had been negotiated long before non-Native people joined the process, and early English, Spanish, and French treaty making often followed Native precedent, focusing their diplomatic efforts on extended discussions that culminated in an oral agreement. Summaries of those agreements were often included in letters or reports made by non-Native people to other interested parties, but the treaty itself was an understanding rather than a document. The Dakota with whom Pike met practiced such diplomacy, and Pike remarked that it "was somewhat difficult to get them to sign the grant, as they conceived the[ir] word of honor should be taken for the Grant, without any Mark." Pike convinced the Dakota to place their marks upon a formal contract by persuading them that it was "not on their account but my own I wanted them to sign." Even among Americans, however, for whom ratification and presidential proclamation were integral parts of the treaty-making process, the agreement was afforded the status of a fully ratified document for many years. Later documents suggest that the treaty's lack of presidential proclamation was genuinely overlooked. Indeed, the treaty was so widely considered to be in effect that when Thomas Forsyth, Indian agent to the Sac and Fox, accompanied Leavenworth on his trip up the Mississippi in 1819, he distributed two thousand dollars in gifts to local Indian communities as he went—the sum Congress decided was sufficient recompense for the land ceded fourteen years before. The United States acted on every front as though the treaty had legal standing.[9]

Entering the region as a man who did not speak the Dakota language, who was confronted with ready evidence of the continued influence of British traders in the region, Leavenworth had orders to *"gain the confidence and friendship of all the Indian tribes with whom you may have any intercourse . . .* [and] hold treaties of friendship with the tribes within our limits." It was, given these circumstances, Leavenworth's personal decision to negotiate for land on which to build a U.S. fort, despite the Pike treaty. Yet his actions were also shaped by more mundane concerns. Three days before the August 9 treaty signing, he had endured a torrential thunderstorm in the inadequate shelter of an ill-constructed log cabin. His company had been drastically depleted by scurvy during the winter of 1819, and he was operating in a region where strong ties to the trade system were the surest avenue to influence and power. Viewed from the vantage point of the banks of the Mississippi River, the U.S. government's belief in its own imperial destiny—and the instruments, like Pike's treaty, that had been put in place to facilitate American ascendancy across the continent—meant little. The United States' goals could not be met by the simple assertion of power and a theoretical cultural superiority. It would take friendship, family connections, and personal relationships between Leavenworth and individuals like Pelagie Faribault for any transformation to take place.[10]

Since her birth in 1783, Pelagie Faribault had been intimately connected to all the groups with whom Leavenworth needed to establish strong relationships in 1820. Although the Upper Midwest was, in the eyes of the U.S. government, a wilderness, the region was in fact fully populated, managed, and used by Native, non-Native, and mixed-heritage communities alike. This was Ojibwe and Dakota country, with the Meskwaki, Ho Chunk, Menominee, and Potawatami as near neighbors. The region had been shaped by 150 years of trade relationships between these communities and European powers, relationships mediated through marriage and structured by the kinship ties that resulted. Through marriage to Native women, traders gained access to a steady supply of furs from their extended Native family and community as well as the vital service of their wives as translators and cultural mediators. In turn, Native communities gained a reliable contact within the trade system, steady access to trade goods, and, by expecting traders to observe kinship rites, protection against egregious abuse. For many years no party involved in this system was able to dominate the other, creating what Richard White has termed a "middle ground" of cultural and economic exchange. In the Upper Midwest that middle ground took on a particularly vibrant shape in the Métis communities at Prairie du Chien, Green Bay, and Pembina. There the mixed-heritage children of trade marriages lived according to cultural standards that were neither wholly Native nor wholly European, wearing clothing that clearly communicated their mixed-heritage identity and participating in the fur trade as brokers and cultural go-betweens in complementary relationships with their Native female relatives.[11]

Pelagie was a child of these cultures, of this time and place. Her father, Joseph Ainse, was the son of French parents, born on Mackinac Island in 1744. Joseph entered the Upper Midwest as a fur trader and fathered Pelagie with a Dakota woman, solidifying his trade connection to his wife's band. Ainse's work was greatly facilitated by the kinship ties he could claim with local Dakota groups, while his ability to speak Dakota and familiarity with Dakota cultural practices helped him land the position of Indian agent under the British. He was called upon to negotiate what peace he could between several Dakota and Ojibwe communities between 1786 and 1787.[12]

Pelagie's own marriage perpetuated these connections between kinship and trade. In 1805, Pelagie married Jean Baptiste Faribault, a French-Canadian born in Berthier, Canada, in 1774. Faribault had entered the fur trade as an employee of the Northwest Fur Company in 1798 and began his career trading at the mouth of the Kankakee River in present-day Illinois. The following year, Faribault relocated to a more western post on the Des Moines River, where his primary trading partners were drawn from Dakota bands. In 1804 Faribault renewed his contract with the Northwest Company, established a post at the juncture of the St. Peter's and Mississippi rivers, and then married Pelagie according to Dakota marital custom.[13]

The glimpses of Pelagie's life that survive in the historical record suggest her importance in facilitating Jean Baptiste's success as a trader. She bore eight children during her marriage, and by the time the 1820 treaty was being negotiated, the eldest, Alexander, was already old enough to assist his father with his fur trade business. In addition, Pelagie and Jean Baptiste often lived apart, a typical arrangement for established fur trade couples. While Jean Baptiste traveled to trade, Pelagie maintained permanent residences with their children on lands at Prairie du Chien, then Pike's Island, and finally at Mendota, the township across the river from Fort Snelling.[14]

Jean Baptiste's prestige in the region owed something to his ability to act as a host to travelers and other traders, an ability that depended on the labor of Pelagie. Whether by reference to the tenets of Euro-American culture, the blended, mixed-heritage communities of the Upper Midwest, or the Dakota community in which she was raised, the nuts and bolts of hospitality—sleeping accommodations and food—were Pelagie's responsibility. There is scattered evidence that suggests she performed this duty skillfully. Fur trader Philander Prescott rested with the Faribaults during a journey upriver in 1820 and enjoyed his welcome to such a degree that he would have stayed longer had he not feared local Native groups (who had set up camp by the Faribault home) would steal the goods he had left outside. In 1819, Colonel Leavenworth also stayed with the Faribault family in Prairie du Chien, and later fondly recalled "the polite and hospitable manner in which I was treated while with you."[15]

We have no way of knowing what interaction existed between Pelagie and Leavenworth during his stay with the family, but it is certain that a friendship flourished between the colonel and Jean Baptiste. Leavenworth recorded that he had learned much about the Dakota from the latter, so much so that he encouraged Jean Baptiste to accompany him upriver as an interpreter and promised him military assistance if he would settle close to the proposed fort. In the period between Leavenworth's departure for the Upper Mississippi and Faribault's move north, Jean Baptiste proved himself even more indispensable to Leavenworth when he directed the colonel to the hemlock which grew at Lake St. Croix. With scurvy decimating his forces, Leavenworth wrote to "assure you that the hemlock is considered of the greatest consequence to us, and the only thing that can save the existence of our men and officers."[16]

By the summer of 1820, then, Leavenworth had incurred an informal debt of gratitude to Jean Baptiste. It was largely because of the latter's help that Leavenworth could claim success in making friendly overtures toward the local Dakota communities. Faribault, through trade and kinship ties, was a known quantity to the Dakota who lived near the St. Peter's and Mississippi rivers—a man who spoke their language, understood their cultural practices, and, through Pelagie, was acknowledged as family. Faribault was more useful to Leavenworth than individuals like Lawrence Taliaferro, the new Indian agent who had arrived in the region with the Fifth Infantry in 1819. Taliaferro's previous experience in the Upper Midwest had been a short stint as a member of the Third Infantry at Chicago in 1816 and an even shorter stint at Green Bay the following year. Despite his commitment to establishing positive relationships between the U.S. government and local Native groups, Taliaferro had no previous experience with the Dakota and could not yet speak their language.[17]

Such was the context in which Leavenworth negotiated with the Dakota on August 9. The treaty, though an imperfect expression of the United States' goals, was made possible by connecting webs of families and friends. Jean Baptiste Faribault occupied a singularly powerful position at the negotiations. His power came not from military might or any particular expression of wealth but from the friendship he had forged with the Fifth Infantry's commanding officer and the cultural and linguistic knowledge he possessed. All these things were made possible by his wife: by her family connections, her language skills, and her labor as a hostess. In effect, Jean Baptiste owed his power to Pelagie, and as a result, it was appropriate in Dakota eyes for her to gain a gift from the proceedings in acknowledgment of *her* work.[18]

The transaction likely looked quite different from Leavenworth's perspective. In Euro-American society, a woman's property became that of her husband on the occasion of their marriage. The laws of coverture suspended a woman's legal identity within that of her husband, granting him control over her land and earnings while they were wed. Within the cultural system Leavenworth best understood, the grant made to Pelagie was in every sense a grant made to her husband; Leavenworth likely expected the land to be governed and controlled by Jean Baptiste. Faribault's contemporaries, as well as subsequent historians, interpreted the grant made to Pelagie Faribault on August 20 in much the same way Leavenworth did; it was a gift to the husband, made through the body of his wife.[19]

Yet Pelagie and Jean Baptiste were not married according to the dictates of Euro-American law. It was as a Dakota woman, married according to the "custom of the country," that Pelagie facilitated Jean Baptiste's entry into Dakota culture. When viewed from within the boundaries of that culture, Pelagie's grant had a particular resonance. It formalized (rather than created) the Faribaults' residency in the area, for while Pelagie had spent most of her married life in Prairie du Chien, her early years had been spent among the Mdewakanton, and her husband frequently lived among the Dakota at the mouth of the St. Peter's as he traded. In addition, the grant (whether Leavenworth understood this or not) acknowledged Dakota cultural practices wherein home and hearth were controlled and owned by women. Tipis and bark lodges, the raw materials used to create clothes and bedding, and the means to process and cook food were all women's purview. The grant of land on which a domestic residence might be established was congruent with gendered Dakota practice.[20]

The 1820 treaty thus captured the complexities of the moment and the fragility of the U.S. position in the Upper Midwest. It pointed to the complicated history of U.S. imperialism in the region since 1805, to the importance of family and friendship in making it possible for Leavenworth to tentatively implement U.S. political goals, and to the power the Dakota retained. Yet even more telling than the situation in 1820 was the situation in 1838, when the U.S. government set about buying Pelagie's land.

While the American population of the region was still small in 1838, it had grown since 1820, and the increases had manifested themselves in very particular ways. The garrison at Fort Snelling was now complete. The stone structure on the bluff overlooking the rivers was capable of sheltering almost 250 members of the Fifth Infantry, plus their families, servants, and slaves. The river valley had become home to American traders such as Henry Sibley and Joseph Brown, traders who had chosen not to enter into lasting "custom of the country" marriages to facilitate their work. A number of missionaries from the American Board of Commissioners for Foreign Missions (ABCFM) had also entered the region, the first in 1829, acting with the blessing of the Department of War and setting up homesteads with the intent of assimilating Native people into American society and converting them to Christianity. As many as 365 civilians lived around the Fort Snelling area: missionaries, employees of the Indian agency, fur traders, early settlers, general laborers, and their families.[21]

Government officials foresaw inevitable conflict between this burgeoning community and local Native groups. They believed, persuaded by their own investment in the concept of "civilization" and swayed by national policy, that by securing land cessions from the Dakota and Ojibwe and restricting Native communities to the west side of the Mississippi River, Americans might settle the region in peace. This approach reflected the specific shift in Indian policy instigated by the Jackson administration and owed much to the fortunes of landholders in the deep South.

On December 20, 1828, soon after Andrew Jackson's successful election to the presidency, the Georgia legislature passed a bill extending the state's jurisdiction over Indian lands within its borders.

The bill was a direct response to the Cherokee's adoption of a constitution in 1827, the most recent of a series of cultural adaptations the Cherokee made in order to provide for their long-term survival and tenure in the region. By 1828 the Cherokee nation boasted a bicameral legislature, a Cherokee alphabet, a bilingual newspaper, their own network of schools and churches, and the flourishing practice of cash-crop agriculture made possible by the labor of slaves. Rather than causing white Georgians to accept the tenure of Indian people on land in their midst, however, such adaptations convinced them that it was imperative to remove Indian people from the state, as the Cherokee showed little sign that they would ever defer to white settlement or governance. Georgian frustration coalesced into a bill passed on December 28 that articulated the state's intent to refuse recognition to Cherokee laws or law enforcement and to make Cherokee citizens liable for taxation. These changes would, the bill stipulated, go into effect on June 1, 1830—a delay designed to give Jackson and Congress time to act upon the issue at a national level.

Jackson was the president of a nation increasingly divided along sectional lines. He could not afford to alienate Georgian support for his administration, especially after the nullification crisis of 1827 demonstrated that there were southern states—South Carolina prime among them—willing to contemplate a vision of national government in which states could pick and choose those aspects of federal governance with which they would comply. Such an approach would necessarily weaken the power of the presidency, and Jackson acted in support of Georgia's ultimatum in part to secure his own power base in Washington, DC. In his first State of the Union address Jackson responded to Georgia's action by committing himself to a policy of removing eastern Native communities from their homelands to territories further west and urged Congress to act on the matter with haste. By February 24, 1830, an Indian Removal bill was out of committee and the subject of fierce debate in Congress. The heat of the debate came from a clash of perspectives over the relative limits of state and federal power. These arguments were directly applicable to the Cherokee case—specifically to Georgia's right, or lack thereof, to govern those living within state limits—but also drew upon larger disagreements about states' rights and the future of slavery in the South. Yet for all their passionate disagreement on the questions of federal and state power, supporters and opponents of the bill alike were in agreement that the government's ultimate goal regarding Indian people was their "civilization." While arguments raged over the meaning of governance in the Republic, all sides agreed that Indian people must inevitably bow before the pressures of American settlement and adapt to American society or die. The rights of white settlers were paramount. As the Cherokees' experience demonstrated, there seemed no definition of the degree of "civilization" that would be enough.[22]

The Removal Act cleared Congress in the spring of 1830, passing the Senate by a majority of 28 to 19 and 102 to 97 in the House. Jackson signed the act into law on May 24, 1830, and threw the weight of the federal government into extinguishing Indian title to land across the South and Midwest. The 1832 Supreme Court decision finding Indian tribes to be "domestic dependent nations"—which affirmed their peculiar sovereignty amid the tug-of-war between state and federal power and suggested the illegality of Georgia and the federal government's acts—did little to alter the path on which Indian affairs had now been launched. For the rest of the century Indian communities would be relocated time and again in the name of civilization.[23]

Aside from these national trends in Indian policy, there were regional and local considerations at play that made land cessions particularly attractive to Americans in the Upper Midwest. The eastern side of the Mississippi River was pine country, and American settlement in upper Illinois and southern Wisconsin had created an insatiable demand for timber to use in construction. Local fur traders favored the negotiation of treaties to help cover the debts incurred by local Indian communities, debts that had escalated as the eastern shores of the Mississippi were overhunted and prices for staples such as muskrat furs tumbled in the East. Native communities came to believe that the annuities and services the treaties offered to them would help mitigate that season's failed wild rice harvest, clear their debts, and aid them in continued tenure on their remaining lands.[24]

These circumstances—national, regional, and local—came together to create the environment in which the U.S. government negotiated treaties with the Dakota and Ojibwe communities holding lands east of the Mississippi River. In return for land cessions and, in the case of the Ojibwe, the protection of their right to hunt, fish, and rice over the ceded territory, the Dakota and Ojibwe were promised financial settlements, tools, cattle, seed, and the assistance of blacksmiths and farmers in practicing "agricultural pursuits." The latter provisions represented a clear attempt on the part of the federal government to pressure the communities into making adaptations to American culture and suggested the increasing power of the United States to dictate the fashion in which the region would develop.[25]

Yet Pelagie's island is a testimony to the uncertainties surrounding U.S. expansion. Since Pelagie was a Dakota woman who had received

Pike's Island as a Dakota gift in an agreement that Congress never ratified, her land occupied a precarious position during treaty negotiations. Although tangible practices—including the construction of Fort Snelling on land demarcated by Leavenworth's treaty—suggested that the agreement was observed in spirit, if not in law, the Faribaults feared that the 1837 treaty might supersede the 1820 agreement, especially since no protective clause suggesting otherwise had been entered into the new document. The Faribaults felt it prudent to engage Samuel Stambaugh and Alexis Bailly (both ex-fur traders, the first a close friend of Jean Baptiste and the second married to the Faribaults' daughter Lucy) to lobby key figures in Washington for the protection of the Pike's Island claim.

Stambaugh and Bailly were successful, impressing upon the secretary of war that Jean Baptiste "is a very respectable old man, a Frenchman, and has resided among that tribe *forty-two* years." As ever, behind the invocation of Faribault's name hovered Pelagie, the lawyers making specific reference to the importance of kinship to the social fabric of the region. "[T]he Ferribault family is the most powerful and influential among the Sioux Indians," wrote Stambaugh to Poinsett in January 1838. "It is families of this description who do much good or much evil among the Indians, with whom they are connected by bonds of blood; and [the] Government would save much blood and treasure, if proper pains were taken to secure their friendship." Poinsett was convinced. Stambaugh and Bailly secured his promise that "the rights of Pelagie Ferribault to the island in question should not be prejudiced by their not being inserted in the treaty." Two things are notable in this promise: Poinsett gave weight to the unratified 1820 agreement, and he did not mention Jean Baptiste's name.[26]

Treaty considerations aside, the government still remained interested in controlling Pike's Island. That interest was twofold: to finish the work of extinguishing all forms of Indian title to lands east of the Mississippi and to meet practical and security needs in controlling land so close to Fort Snelling. As Stambaugh described it, "the head of the island is separated from the walls of the fort by a small slough, about fifty yards, in width . . . [B]y damming this slough, or throwing a wall across it at both ends, the island can be made a part of the main land." Taliaferro claimed he had, as early as 1820, suggested to Leavenworth that "in times of difficulty or danger from the tribes, the post would require the island (though small) as a place of safety for the public cattle and horses (being directly under the guns of the fort.)" In 1838 Major Joseph Plympton, the commanding officer of the fort, wrote that the military should "embrace Pike's Island, which I consider to be of *vital* important to this Fort as a pasture." While pasture might seem a mundane consideration, livestock were often targeted by local Native groups during periods of hostility. The loss of milk and beef cattle was a particularly troubling prospect for a fort still dependent on external suppliers for most of its subsistence needs.[27]

Convinced of the island's value to the military, Congress took up the issue of the Faribaults' claim in 1838, and on April 25 a joint resolution authorized the secretary of war to contract with the Faribaults for the purchase of Pelagie's land. Poinsett finalized negotiations with the Faribaults on March 12, 1839, agreeing to purchase the island for $12,000, (about $239,000 today), subject to congressional approval. No objection was raised by the War Department or Congress to Pelagie's ownership of the land despite her status as a married woman. A Euro-American woman of the same era could be gifted property while she was married, but the property would only remain hers (as opposed to her husband's) if her family could afford to create a trust for the property's protection. It would be many years before a married Anglo woman could independently sell, contract, or rent out her own land. Pelagie's ownership of Pike's Island, however, depended upon her being Dakota; at least part of her value as a marital partner rested on the same. She lived outside the boundaries of coverture, had been married by the custom of her own community, and owned all that related to the home. By their actions, the men who sat in judgment upon Pelagie's case upheld Dakota gender practice, regardless of their intellectual and ideological understanding of Dakota and Euro-American marital law.[28]

The decision was not met happily at Fort Snelling. Lawrence Taliaferro immediately wrote to the secretary of war, arguing that Dakota title to the land had been extinguished by Pike's treaty in 1805, and—even if that agreement were overlooked—completely extinguished by the treaties of 1837. Taliaferro rounded out his tally of offenses by bringing up the issue of residency: no one had made a permanent home on the island for fifteen years. Major Plympton, the commanding officer of Fort Snelling, sided with Taliaferro, adding that Jean Baptiste was a Canadian and "alien," and forwarded a letter he had received from Taliaferro in which the latter pointed out that Jean Baptiste had no claim to the land before 1820: he had not taken up residence on the island until after Leavenworth had suggested he do so.[29]

Taliaferro and Plympton's arguments were made squarely from within the tenets of Euro-American culture. They focused their objections on Jean Baptiste, criticizing any claim he could make to the island on the basis of his citizenship and residency. They neither acknowledged nor tackled the question of *Pelagie's* ownership of the land or the fact that she had maintained residency there in Jean Baptiste's absence until a flood made the island uninhabitable in 1822. Taliaferro and Plympton did their best to make Pelagie disappear. The woman that emerged from their discussions of the island was a woman with no control over her property, a woman subject to the structures of coverture. This tactic not only served them in trying to argue that the Faribaults should not be made rich by the island's sale but reflected their larger attempts to stamp the social relations of Euro-American society on the region. The inhabitants of the region, however, were not so malleable, even on paper, as the Indian agent and commanding officer of the fort might wish.

There was policy, there were ideals, and then there was the reality of the national colonial venture. All the parties who worked for the U.S. government—Plympton, Taliaferro, Poinsett, and commissioner of Indian affairs T. Hartley Crawford—agreed that Pike's Island was a valuable, even necessary holding for Fort Snelling. Yet while Plympton and Taliaferro argued that the U.S. government should ignore the 1820 agreement and simply act as if the land belonged to the state, those officers of the government stationed in Washington had a different assessment of the situation. Eyeing the unrest among midwestern Indian groups, understanding the scarcity of game in the area, mindful of the power of traders to influence relationships with local Native communities, and—crucially—with no personal investment in the rapid ascendancy of American systems of government near the fort, Crawford and Poinsett acknowledged that the United States did not yet posses the power required to dictate the outcome it wanted in the Pike's Island matter. In Crawford's own words, "As a principle of general observance, the United States, in my judgement, cannot recognize such grants [as were made to Pelagie Faribault] . . . This case, however, occupies a position of its own . . . The island is wanted for the purposes of the Government. To avoid delay, and difficulty, and controversy, it may be judicious . . . to purchase it. All Indian claim will be put at rest."[30]

It would be many more years before the U.S. government paid the Faribault family for Pelagie's island. (Pelagie herself died in 1847.) An act of Congress was required for the appropriation of the funds to fulfill the 1839 agreement, and, in Crawford's words, "the requisition was made too late for the action of [the 25th] Congress." The matter was referred back to Congress during the next session and passed in the Senate but was "lost in the House of Representatives, with several other amendments to the appropriation bill, on the last day of the session." Congress considered the matter but took no definitive action in 1842; the same was true in 1846. Though no record of Pelagie's claim appeared in the journals of either house again until 1855, in 1857 Senator Jones of Tennessee remarked that the matter was "an old acquaintance of everybody who has been in the Senate during the last fourteen years." Both houses of Congress wrestled with the claim between 1855 and 1857, and in 1858 the Treasury Department finally issued payment in the sum of $12,000.[31]

That the settlement received increased attention in the 1850s is most likely owed to congressional interest in reducing the size of the Fort Snelling military reserve. The reserve's boundaries had been fixed in 1837 when, in tacit acknowledgment of the imprecision of Pike's treaty, the adjutant general ordered Major Plympton to map that land he deemed necessary to the garrison's military needs.

Plympton's map was expansive, delineating a reserve that stretched for twenty miles—necessary, Plympton argued, for cattle and timber and to prevent whiskey peddlers from setting up shop close to the garrison. The reserve did not encompass the Falls of St. Anthony, though it did take in the land above, as well as every possible steamboat landing for fifteen miles below. The adjutant general accepted the boundaries that Plympton suggested, and even before approval was sent back from Washington Plympton set about removing settlers from the reserve. The previously thriving community around the fort—estimated to be 157 individuals with two hundred horses and cattle—dissipated, and without good river transportation available for nonmilitary purposes the reserve became, in the words of one local trader, "a source of serious annoyance to the business operations of the country." By the 1850s settlers had found other places to do business—St. Paul had become the commercial and political hub of the territory. This, along with the cession of Dakota lands in the treaties of 1851, convinced Congress that there was little need for a large military installation in Minnesota. Congress reduced the boundaries of the reserve in 1852, and in 1853 settlers were permitted to move into those areas that had previously been controlled by the military. By 1857 the government was actively looking to sell the garrison. It can be of little surprise that in this atmosphere Samuel Stambaugh was dispatched to protect Pelagie's claim once again, lest the government try to divest itself of land for which it had not yet paid.[32]

Pelagie's claim had support in Congress from those who considered payment a matter of honoring an established debt. In its report on the claim on February 9, 1855, the Senate Committee on Military Affairs unanimously recommended that Jean Baptiste and Pelagie receive $12,000 "in fulfillment of the contract of March 12, 1839." The claim came to the House as part of the Indian appropriation bill later that month, and in debate, Representative Brekenridge of Kentucky concurred with the Senate's opinion. "It was stipulated in the contract" of 1839, he argued, "that if the appropriation was not made at the next session of Congress, the contract should be declared void. The appropriation was not made, but, so far from the contract being declared void, the United States have held, and still hold, the property in their possession." Representative Haven of New York added further detail. "Mr. Poinsett advised the Faribaults, or their agents, by letter, that they had better not treat the contract as at an end," he recounted, "that he would call the attention of Congress to the matter again." After much debate the House declined the Senate's amendment to the appropriation bill but passed its own. In conference both chambers agreed on an amendment supporting payment of a claim, with an added provision, in deference to those members of Congress who were unsure of the details in the matter, that "the Secretary of War shall be satisfied with the validity of their title to the lands mentioned in said contract, and that the conveyance to the United States be made sufficient to pass the said title."[33]

Jefferson Davis, the secretary of war, was unpersuaded of Pelagie's claim. Davis suggested that it was invalid because the island had been ceded to the United States in Pike's 1805 treaty. Furthermore, he argued, even if that treaty had no standing, the 1820 treaty on which Pelagie's claim depended had never been ratified by Congress. Stambaugh—incensed, if his use of italics and block capitals are anything to go by—took to print in response, publishing a thirty-six-page defense of Pelagie's claim in 1856. He swiftly dispatched with Davis's first objection, itemizing the irregularities surrounding Pike's treaty. On his second point, Stambaugh argued, the secretary quite misunderstood the nature of what had happened at Camp Coldwater in 1820. The sections of the treaty relating to Pelagie's island recorded a transaction between Dakota people—the approval of the United States was neither sought nor necessary, and it was a mere accident that the kind of gift that had long been a feature of Dakota life was written down by an American scribe. "[T]he title of that grant, *by the Sioux tribe of Indians*, TO A WOMAN OF THAT TRIBE, is as *good* and *valid* a title as can be made by a tribe of Indians, and must remain so until annulled or rescinded by the *grantors!*" he argued. No one had extinguished the Dakota title to the island, and Pelagie's ownership had been protected by Poinsett during the treaty negotiations of 1837. As such she had a perfect right to possess and sell the island as she wished.[34]

Stambaugh was correct: the transaction that netted Pelagie her island was an agreement between Dakota people, but this was a truth that few in Washington could grasp as they saw Pelagie, first and foremost, as a married woman. As such, members of the military and of Congress assumed that coverture governed the transaction and that Pelagie's island belonged to Jean Baptiste. In all the congressional debates surrounding the island in the 1850s, the matter was referred to as the claim of Jean B., John, or J. Bte and Pelagie Faribault. Representative Haven of New York characterized the government's 1839 agreement to buy the island as being with "this man Faribault, and Pelagie Faribault," while the relevant amendment to the Indian Appropriations Act of 1855 held that Poinsett had contracted, in 1839, with "Jean B. Faribault and Pelagie, his wife." While such a characterization of the claim might be supposed to reflect Congress's understanding that Pelagie was dead and Jean Baptiste was her heir, evidence from the debates suggest this detail was not part of the equation—indeed, the House of Representatives seemed to know little about the case, including such key details as whether Fort Snelling stood on Pelagie's island or beside it. In debates in 1857, Senator Bell of Tennessee was particularly direct in suggesting that Jean Baptiste was the owner of the island, suggesting that the United States had agreed to "make a concession to this old Indian, Faribault, or some member of his family." Stambaugh had no doubt that both Congress and the secretary of war were looking for ownership in all the wrong places. "The 'grant' or 'gift' or 'reservation' of the island was not made to J. B. Ferribault, a *Canadian Frenchman,*' as he has been designated, but to *Pelagie Ferribault, a Sioux Indian woman!*" he fumed.[35]

In the end, the presumption of coverture was superseded by notions of honor among members of Congress. Senator Bell of Tennessee, himself a former secretary of war, suggested that Secretary Davis was tarnishing the reputation of the United States in refusing to honor agreements made by his predecessors. "I remember that the question was referred to me when I had the honor, or the misfortune, for a short time to occupy the post of Secretary of War," he recalled. "I investigated it thoroughly, and I considered that the faith of the Government had been pledged by my predecessor, as well as by the original contract with these parties. I thought it was not a question for us to decide, whether or not we should comply with the treaty." Senator Weller of California was even more forceful: "You have taken possession of the lands of these Indians; and now you refuse to pay them the money, or give them back the lands, and that you call good faith! The Indians were in peaceful possession of this property; you wanted it for military purposes; you agreed to give them $12,000 if they would surrender it to you; they did surrender it, you took possession, established your military post there, and then you will not allow them to have the money which you stipulated to pay, nor will you give them back the land!" Chastened, the Senate passed the bill 31 to 7.[36]

In 1858, Pelagie's heirs received $12,000 from the U.S. government in payment for land that their mother had owned outright her entire life. Pelagie Faribault occupied a legal, social, and cultural space quite different from the standard Euro-American model that existed in 1820, 1838, or 1858. Her ownership of Pike's Island was an extension of the particular circumstances of the Upper Midwest, with its multiplicity of cultures and their ideas about gendered behavior and the meaning of land. Yet that story is easily missed if we prioritize the thoughts, actions, and life stories of men over women, literate over illiterate, military over civilian, and Americans over the Dakota and their mixed-heritage descendents. The narrative of American expansionism is often defined by those who, because of race, gender, wealth, and education, stood most ready to record their participation in the process, resulting in an uncomplicated story that suggests—erroneously—how easily the Midwest was won. Moving Pelagie Faribault to the center of the narrative changes that story. It reveals the uneven application of imperialism's tenets in the region, the necessity of the American system adapting, for a time, to the cultural landscape of the Dakota, and the power that individuals, too often considered uniformly powerless, could claim in that mix.

Elsewhere, other Dakota communities were also negotiating the presence of non-Native people in their midst, as well as the differing ideas about family and community they carried with them. The missionaries of the American Board of Commissioners for Foreign

Missions were one such group of outsiders who, beginning in 1829, set their sights on the Upper Midwest. The missionaries believed they understood what constituted civilized, moral behavior, and set out to persuade Native communities of the same. Marital practice— who could marry, how, and with what consequence—was central to that endeavor, but as missionary Mary Riggs discovered, marriage was a locus of Native resistance to "civilization" as much as a site of potential social change.

GUARDING THE CORN FIELDS

Dakota women were the agriculturalists of their communities, which meant not only growing crops but protecting the fields from predators.

CHAPTER TWO

Marriage among the Missionaries

ETWEEN FEBRUARY 1837 and January 1838, Mary Ann Longley bore repeated witness to the importance of marriage among the numerous communities of the Upper Midwest. Her own marriage to Ohio-born clergyman Stephen Riggs on February 16, 1837, began the process—Riggs had contracted to take up mission work among the Dakota at Lac qui Parle, three hundred miles west of Fort Snelling. The newlywed couple arrived at the fort on June 1, 1837, and on June 24 Stephen gave a closing prayer at the Christian marriage of Philander Prescott, a trader, to Nah-he-no-Wenah, his Dakota companion of many years. It was September before the Riggses reached their own mission station, and there, on November 1, Stephen presided over the marriage of missionaries Sarah Poage and Gideon Pond. There were still more marriages in the offing: on December 25, Big Thunder's son was married to Sparkling Iron in the Dakota village near Mary's home, and on January 11, 1838, the daughter of trader Joseph Renville married a French fur trader in a ceremony conducted entirely in Dakota and French.[1]

Mary was witness to the fact that marriage—an economic and almost always sexual partnership sealed by the exchange of goods, homes, vows, and sometimes names—encapsulated central truths about each cultural group that met in the Upper Midwest. Each community maintained a specific sense of what marriage meant, how it should be celebrated, and what responsibilities were inherent in its practice: marriage provided a blueprint for social cohesion. For both the Christian missionaries of the American Board of Commissioners for Foreign Missions (ABCFM) and the Dakota and Ojibwe communities that they sought to convert, marriage was a spiritual matter, a labor agreement, an indicator of social status, and—hopefully—a means to assure companionship. Yet these similarities were not always visible to each group. The Dakota people who came and went from the camping grounds at Lac qui Parle expressed no opinion of Christian marriage of which the missionaries themselves were aware. The missionaries, however, found much to condemn in Dakota marriage, from ceremonies to polygamy to the division of labor between men and women. Neither group changed the other, however—the Dakota because they did not care to, and the missionaries because they had no power to effect the alterations they so desperately desired.

The ability of each of the communities Mary observed to marry as they pleased tells us much about the power of the encroaching American state. The Dakota among whom Mary lived wanted no part of the Americans' marital practices and through mid-century had the power to resist attempts to make them adopt them. The American missionaries judged Dakota practices but could do little more than lament what they saw—this was not yet an American place. Yet changes were occurring in the marital fabric of the region. Whereas

marriages according to the "custom of the country" had long flourished in the Upper Midwest, fur traders began in the 1830s to solemnize their unions according to American practice. With more
Euro-Americans arriving in the Upper Midwest, trader marriages
began to turn toward the structures of that community, hinting at the
cultural and political changes the region was soon to face.

Marriage—the prospect of her own and that of others—had provided structure to Mary Longley's world long before she wed Stephen
Riggs at the age of twenty-two. In the summer of 1833, aged nine-
teen, she was witness to her sister's "sacrifice at Hymen's altar," a
marriage that Mary lamented to her brother Alfred, writing that
she could not "endure the thought that L[ucretia] will there vow to
love another better than she does us." Mary was, herself, entertaining
suitors and found the process discomfiting. "I do not expect a 'suitor
knight' although to me those days of chivalry have seemed replete
with the scenes of the most bewitching romance," she wrote Alfred.
"I am far yes very far from wishing the customs of those days trans-
ferred to the present age, yet think a little of the gallantry of older
time would render many a social circle more interesting and many a
young monsieur Chase more *tolerable*." In Alfred's opinion, Mary
was best suited to "living a life of 'single blessedness,'" and her actions
perhaps gave weight to such a point of view. Rather than marrying
any of the Messieurs Chase in her social circle, Mary became a stu-
dent at Ipswich Female Seminary and gave serious contemplation to
missionary work. Even then, questions of marriage were inescapable.
"Having had the destitute & ignorant state of females in Illinois pre-
sented by Miss Grant," she wrote her brother in November 1834,

"I cannot but feel or desire to do something to rescue them from ignorance so degrading. It was stated as a fact that the females marry young & totally ignorant of the duties of a wife."[2]

Whatever romantic ideals Mary had once found alluring, she had by the age of twenty-one decided to teach where she could do, in her own estimation, the most good, embracing "none of the romance but much of the reality of life." It was in this period that Mary met Stephen Riggs. In February 1836 she was twenty-two years old, a teacher in Bethlehem, Indiana, and far from her family home in Hawley, Massachusetts. On February 2 of that year, Mary wrote to tell her mother of a letter received from Reverend Dyer Burgess, the clergyman who had acted as her "protector" on her journey west in 1835. He wrote now to introduce "a friend of his, a man of promising talents now a member of the Western Theological Seminary preparing for a mission to China." The friend, wrote Mary, had asked Burgess "to ascertain whether I was under any particular engagement and provided I was not . . . [he] would visit Indiana in April." Mary regarded the proposition as a serious matter, less because of the prospect of marriage itself than because of the work her marriage might sustain. "I shall decide nothing regarding the individual alluded to at present," she wrote her brother Alfred, "but I ought soon to decide regarding my own duty—my fitness for a missionary."[3]

Stephen Riggs's visit to Bethlehem in April deepened Mary's contemplation of the spiritual duty inherent in the marriage he proposed. "You know I despise the affectation of romance and desire to bring my views down to sober reality," she wrote to Alfred after Riggs's departure. Yet even in a marriage premised upon service to God, Mary felt sure there should be amiability between partners, and on this point she had qualms. "I think him, viz. Mr. Riggs, intelligent, well informed and deeply interested in the cause of missions," she wrote, "but as yet I do not feel that regard which I am sure I ought to feel for a lone fellow pilgrim." She described Riggs as "one smaller than middle stature, plainer than the mediocrity, even very homely if you please & appearing to better advantage in conversation than in the desk [pulpit]." She tried to consider what extenuating circumstances might have affected the manner of their meeting. "Though Mr. R. seemed familiar yet there was not that frankness, that open heartedness, which I had hoped for. It might have been occasioned by my own demeanor, for notwithstanding all resolutions I had formed of forgetting my old aversion to introductions, & thinking only of the great & blessed work in contemplation, it would occasionally force itself upon me," she wrote. Riggs had promised to write letters, and Mary hoped they would be "frank and explicit." In the interim she planned to "commune with my own heart, listen to the 'still and small voice' & obey its dictates." Personal compatibility was of less importance to Mary than discerning the will of God.[4]

Riggs shared Mary's faith that God would reveal the proper course of action regarding their potential marriage. "I know if I trust God I cannot be disappointed in a companion," he wrote to Mary in May. Riggs believed that God would make him a good husband and that as a husband he would do God's work. "I would entirely trust His goodness to provide me with such a [wife]," he wrote, "& enable me also to be such a one as will promote happiness & advance His cause." Like Mary, Riggs's decision making was practical rather than sentimental. "I know you love the poor," he wrote. "I should think from your conversation that you would have very little difficulty in deciding that it is your duty to become a missionary—but this will scarce touch the question whether you are willing to go with me."

Mary forwarded the letter to her mother, noting that "I shall content myself if he has good common sense, is kind & a devoted Christian." By June Mary had accepted Riggs's proposal.[5]

The Riggses' marriage ceremony affirmed the spiritual nature of their commitment to one another, to God, and to their families. A year into their marriage, Mary wrote a poem for Stephen reminiscing about their wedding day:

> Our marriage day I too remember well
> And all its scenes, its scenes of interest deep—
> Our friends and kindred dear—the ancient church
> The messenger of God—the silent throng—
> And music sweet, are fresh in memory still.
> Again that day has dawned on us, so bright
> And beautiful.
> Let us give thanks to God.
> For all the blessings strewed along our path
> Since it was one, and I was what I am yr. wife.[6]

Although there is no record of the exact liturgy used at Mary and Stephen's wedding, the conventions of Protestant wedding ceremonies were remarkably similar across denominational lines. The ceremony identified God as the means by which two individuals became one—the joiner or "knytt[er]" of souls. His will superseded that of any other, making the marriage a lifelong connection that no human being could end. The ceremony also formally recognized the separation of children from parents, whether by the "giving" of the bride by her father or the Biblical exhortation for a man to leave his parents and take a wife. One family life came to an abrupt end upon marriage, but another began: the ceremony reminded a couple that marriage was in part ordained so that children could be raised in the sight of God. The theme of separation was inherent in a Christian, Euro-American marriage ceremony: separation from individualism, from a person's family of birth, and from worldly temptations. This theme of separation was particularly significant for Stephen and Mary, poised to begin a journey into the Upper Midwest.[7]

Yet religious rites, music, and a gathering of friends and family did not make a marriage legal. Massachusetts required that before a wedding could take place, prospective couples must publish their intent to marry on three separate occasions at a church or the offices of the town clerk. The wedding must be presided over by a designated representative of the state of Massachusetts—it was as such a figure, rather than as a man of God, that the clergyman who married Mary and Stephen gave legal weight to the proceedings. Finally, the marriage had to be recorded by the minister and that record turned over to the town clerk: failure to do this would have the minister stripped of his ability to marry others. When these requirements were met, couples became man and wife, assuming the specific roles and responsibilities inherent in coverture and their designated, gendered relationships to the state. These elements did not make it into Mary's poem but they were nevertheless the reason she was married in the eyes of the law.[8]

Mary and Stephen were not alone in considering duty to God to be of particular importance in undertaking marriage—other ABCFM missionaries in the Upper Midwest expressed similar ideas. William Boutwell of the ABCFM Ojibwe missions married Hester Crooks in September 1834, an action he reported to his superiors in Boston in January of the following year. He needed help with the physical labor involved in establishing a mission station at Leech Lake and was concerned that the Ojibwe might think him in need of a Native wife if he lived alone. "[W]hat was my duty?" Boutwell wrote. "I cast my [eye] over the barren desolate land, & asked, is there a helper?" God's answer was, he believed, direct. "Instead of going into the first lodge I should chance to fall upon & throwing down my blanket, Prov. Directed me to send a dispatch 3 days march across the wilderness to Yellow Lake with proposals to Miss Hester Crooks." Granville Sproat, also of the Ojibwe missions, likewise deferred to God in the business of choosing a wife. Sproat, who set out to find a companion in 1837, did so because it was "the opinion of my brethren in the field that I can best glorify God and make myself useful among the heathen by such a course." Sproat's search for a worthy candidate took him to Mackinaw, Detroit, and finally to his home town of Middleborough in New England. From there he wrote to David Greene, secretary of the ABCFM, with an eleven-point manifesto listing the qualities he thought a missionary wife should possess. All, save one, detailed spiritual characteristics and a mindfulness of the soul's duty to God. His last point was more down to earth: a wife should have a "well disciplined mind, together with a good domestic education," he wrote.[9]

"A good domestic education" was of critical necessity to the missions at large: marriage secured to each husband, and the mission to which he was attached, the female labor so vital to the running of a household and community. Stephen Riggs's initial inquiry into Mary's marital state came not because of a personal relationship between the two but because Riggs believed that a wife was a necessary help in mission work. This belief, whether based upon his familiarity with other mission enterprises or merely with family labor in general, was shared by other missionaries in the Upper Midwest. In one of his many letters decrying the labor shortages at the ABCFM mission at La Pointe, missionary Sherman Hall was blunt: "We need a man who is married, or at least, we need female help in this mission." David Greene articulated much the same sentiment in a letter to Indian agent Henry Schoolcraft in 1833, writing that the mission at La Pointe would ideally include "our ordained missionary & his wife, with an interpreter, a female teacher, & perhaps another female helper." In 1834, S. B. Munger wrote to David Greene to ask if the board could supply a woman who would enter the mission enterprise with him should he accept the board's proposal to move west. Greene replied that the board knew of "no female helper" and advised that "it would be better for you to have one with whom you are acquainted . . . whom you expect will accompany you as your wife." In 1835 William Boutwell continued the theme, arguing that all mission families should include one man and two women (except where this might be misinterpreted as polygamy among local Native groups). In a letter to Samuel Pond of the Dakota missions that same year, Boutwell made it clear that taking a wife was at least in part meant to fulfill the labor needs of the mission station. "I expected help from the Board last season, but they could not or did not help me, so I helped myself and took a wife," he wrote.[10]

A lack of sufficient female labor could exact a heavy cost upon the mission stations. Jedediah Stevens, missionary to the Dakota at Lake Harriet, petitioned Greene for more help at the mission in 1838, arguing that his wife and sister-in-law "were sinking under the weight of the *care* and labour [*sic*] devolving upon *them*." Similarly, when forced to do without the labor of his wife during her protracted illness in 1834, Sherman Hall of the mission at La Pointe wrote of his "time of solicitude and trial": "We were unable to procure any domestic help, or any one to relieve us for a single night watching [over the sick bed]," he wrote to David Greene. Faced with the care of a four-month-old child who could no longer be breast-fed and with the wife of their neighbor—a potential source of domestic support—also ill, he wrote, "we knew not what to do." Ojibwe missionary L. H. Wheeler had an able wife, yet wrote to his superiors in 1843, asking "if the Board can send us some pious female, who will be willing come here and labor *cheerfully* as domestic help," thereby reducing the arduous labor his wife undertook. He also had other tasks in mind. "In addition to her duties in the family she might be useful in the S. School, prayer meeting, and in various other ways," he wrote. "Could she *sing*, it would be quite an additional aid."[11]

The duties of missionary wives were numerous. Jedediah Stevens described his wife's role as "keeping the house in order and providing food and clothing washing &c for the members of the family, and treating with bare civility the numerous calls we have from the Garrison, trading posts, and other mission stations and from abroad . . . [A]ll this must be done with from one, to a dozen Indians constantly soliciting some little deed of charity, or act of kindness, which is enough to occupy the time of one individual at least." Florantha Thompson, the young woman who agreed to become Granville Sproat's wife, wrote to her mother that "I am my own servant. I have no one to assist me . . . I scour my own knifes, candlesticks and tin pans, which is no small job." Household production was central to the labor women performed—dipping candles, making soap, turning raw fabric into clothing, and, in Florantha's words, making "my own butter which is considerable having only one cow. We are very fond of Dutch cheese in the making of which I use all my bonny-clabber."

At a time when the American Board frequently complained of insufficient finances—"pecuniary embarrassments" in the words of David Greene—women's labor added economic value to the supplies each mission station received. Without women's labor there would have been flour but no bread; pork but no stew; wicks but no candles; yarn but no socks.[12]

Stephen and Mary Riggs participated in a labor system at Lac qui Parle which was, as at all the region's mission stations, deeply gendered. Farmer Alexander Huggins managed the agricultural operations of the station, raising hay, corn, potatoes, and turnips as well as caring for the cattle. Both Riggs and Thomas Williamson, the ordained clergymen of the mission, were expected to assist Huggins and also to construct buildings, study Dakota, translate the Bible into Dakota, conduct Sunday services, control the mission budget, order supplies, and report their progress to the ABCFM in Boston. Assistant Gideon Pond, while spending most of his time studying Dakota, was expected "to work with Mr. Huggins when necessary and . . . [to] perform labor enough, to remunerate us for his board and clothing." Beyond their mission responsibilities there were chores reserved for men in each household—Stephen particularly remembered the difficulty of supplying enough chopped wood to keep his family warm through winter. Mary Riggs, Margaret Williamson, Sarah Poage Pond, and Lydia Huggins all shouldered the domestic labor for their respective families. Before meals could be cooked, foodstuffs had to be processed. Turnips and potatoes were pulled, washed, and chopped, corn dried and ground in a hand mill to provide the basis for hominy or rough bread, and wild fowl plucked. Mary wrote her mother with pride after learning to make soap with lye and grease, but wash day annoyed her to such a degree that unlike her neighbors, she hired a succession of Dakota women to take up the task. (Her own distaste for doing laundry did not stop Mary complaining about the job done by the Dakota women she hired.) The mission women knitted, sewed, and wove their own cloth, taught English, math, and American ideas of domesticity in school, and were the chief nurses and midwives at the station. The care of children also fell upon their shoulders.[13]

Isolation from wider American society provided some small opportunities for mission couples to define marital work roles in new ways, as the Riggses' struggle to milk their cow demonstrates. Mary "grew up in New England, where men alone did the milking, and I in Ohio, where the women alone milked in those days," recalled Riggs. "At first it took both to milk a cow, and it was poorly done. But Mary succeeded best. Nevertheless, application and perseverance succeeded, and, although never boasting of any special ability in that line of things, I could do my own milking." Aside from preserving the comical machinations of two individuals at odds with their cow, Riggs's story reveals much about gender conventions at Lac qui Parle. There was no one at the mission site who cared to tell Mary she was doing a man's job, nor to mock Stephen for taking on a task reserved for women. In the absence of societal instruction one way or another, the couple chose the route that suited them best—Mary was more skilled and would milk the cow most often, but Stephen could get by in a pinch. Necessity also expanded the other roles of husband and wife from time to time. While construction was Stephen's job— he built the bed on which he and Mary slept—Mary joined him in winterizing the inside of their rooms before the year's end.[14]

For the Riggses, marriage was a legal contract and spiritual compact given meaning by the day-to-day exchange of services and responsibilities between man and wife. They believed themselves to be "in the wilds of the West," and within that framing their marriage gained its meaning from a shared sense of purpose—to Christianize the Dakota—and the practical work it took to realize that goal. Mary confessed to her mother in October 1837 that she found the Dakota language difficult to learn, that her duties in the home took more time than she had imagined, and that with the imminent birth of her first child she worried that she was "insufficient for these things." Nevertheless, she reflected, "when I feel as though the prospect of my being able to do much for these Indians is the darkest, it affords me pleasure to think that perhaps I may enable my dear husband to do more than he could do alone."[15]

For the Dakota, marriage was not simply a compact between husband and wife but an agreement affirming the importance of kinship and community as a whole. Mary Riggs understood little of this when she observed some of the practices involved in the beginning of a new marriage in 1837. "Last Saturday," she wrote on January 1, 1838, "a son of Big Thunder a Dakota Chief 'took a wife' by making her father a liberal present, which consisted of five guns, a cow, leggins, breech cloth, & blanket. The father, approving, accepted the present by firing the guns & his daughter was a wife." Mary thought herself witness to the purchase of a wife, as if women were pots or blankets to be bought from a trader. Instead she had caught a glimpse of the ties between families that were cemented by Dakota marriage—the building and strengthening of a web of kinship that governed all of Dakota life.[16]

From birth, Dakota children were surrounded by a vast kinship network. Relatives linked to an individual through marriage were as important as relatives linked through blood ties. A child's fathers included the biological parent and also the father's brothers and male

cousins; similarly, the sisters and female cousins of a child's biological mother were also considered mothers to the child. A child
also had aunts and uncles—the sisters of his or her biological father
and the brothers of his or her biological mother. All the children of
a child's mothers and fathers were considered siblings; the children
of aunts and uncles considered cousins. This kin network expanded
even further upon marriage. The new relatives of an aunt or uncle,
for example, became the child's relatives, too.[17]

"[R]elationships through marriage extend practically ad infini-
tum," wrote Dakota anthropologist Ella Deloria in 1944, and as such
offered protection to the community from outsiders. The Dakota
addressed each other in familial terms, establishing both their connection and the social practices inherent in such a relationship. Anyone who could not establish a kinship tie, "no matter how torturous,"
was an outsider and not to be trusted. Adoption mitigated this practice by creating fictive kinship ties among individuals and endowing
each with reciprocal obligations toward the other.[18]

Marriage rites highlighted the importance of kinship within the
Dakota community. Amos Oneroad, a Sisseton-Wahpeton man
whose maternal great-grandfather lived at Lac qui Parle in 1838,
offered a detailed description of marriage practices among the
Sisseton-Wahpeton Dakota in a manuscript he wrote in the 1920s.
Once a couple felt sure of their mutual affection, he wrote, a "boy's
father or an old man hired by him would take a pipe of tobacco to
the girl's parents and ask for her." If the proposal was accepted, "the
older people" smoked while the girl dressed and painted a red spot
on each cheek. When ready, the girl mounted her parents' best horse
and was led to her prospective husband's home by her male relatives, where a feast was prepared and the bride was received by female

members of the groom's family. The bride's relatives challenged any other man present to claim her, then "fired their guns, refused the feast offered them, and went back [to their own family] . . . [A]fter this, the groom's family went to the girl's parents carrying hides and garments to give to the sisters or cousins of the girl." The rites ended with a giveaway of food and presents to relatives and the poor.[19]

It took an extensive number of family members from all generations to formalize a marriage, affirming the interconnectedness of the kinship group. It was the job of the groom's female relations to work the hides that would be offered to the bride's family, for example, and the women of both families would have been responsible for cooking the feasts. By issuing a challenge at the groom's home, the bride's male relatives were staking their honor upon their belief that she was fit for marriage: had someone come forward to claim her—had she been engaged in some other relationship—it would have been a sharp blow to the status of her entire family. The marriage rites also acted as instruction from one generation to the next, reminding the young couple to be hospitable, generous, and mindful of their kin. Tellingly, the rites did not automatically involve the removal of the couple to their own home. Inclusion, not separation, stood at the heart of Dakota marriage.[20]

The Dakota observed a division of labor between men and women in which husbands and wives contributed to the total workload of their camp circle as well as the needs of their individual household. Men were responsible for hunting large and small game, plus muskrat in the winter for trading purposes. In the turbulent late 1830s, men from the bands around Lac qui Parle were increasingly involved in warfare against the Ojibwe as well as acting as diplomats and councilmen both inside the community and in the community's dealings with the U.S. government and its representatives. Women were responsible for farming; for processing the meat and hides from game; for the upkeep of tipis, summer camping lodges, and maple sugar shacks; for the transportation of home and household effects on the hunt; for cooking, cleaning, and gathering; and for offering constant hospitality, including food, to expected and unexpected guests alike.[21]

This division of labor in Dakota marriages caused great consternation among the missionaries at Lac qui Parle. The focus of male missionaries was on Dakota men, judging them idle beggars who were too proud to farm. Mary Riggs, on the other hand, paid close attention to Dakota women's work. She considered their lot in life pitiable and confided to her mother in 1839 that she could not "endure [to see] such slavery as we see day to day." Armed with their own understanding of the labor most appropriate for men and women, the missionaries consistently misunderstood what they saw.[22]

The most common charge laid against Dakota men by the missionaries was that they were idle and begged because they would not exert themselves to properly provide for their families. Thomas Williamson wrote with some frustration in 1839, "When we are hard at work to provide for ourselves food and other necessaries and a parcel of idle fellows who for weeks have been doing nothing but playing sleeping eating and smoking come lounging about us and begging us for food and other things it is natural to tell them that if they would do as we do they might provide food for themselves." Mary Riggs concurred, remarking one afternoon that same year, "After being quite tired with continued begging for a little milk and bread . . . I went to sit with Mrs. Huggins awhile, feeling considerably discouraged by new manifestations of the pride and laziness of men and boys." "Although there are many Indian men who think they cannot dig," she had confided to her brother Thomas in 1838, "there are very few who would be ashamed to beg."[23]

For the missionaries, this perceived "idleness" was compounded by the tasks that then fell to Dakota women. Mary Riggs greatly pitied Sparkling Iron her marriage on December 25, 1838, believing the young woman to be entering a life of servitude, cutting wood and carrying burdens. "An Indian woman may hoe & chip, or pack burdens large enough for an ox or horse while her lord & master walks near with his gun & possibly some other trifle," she wrote in 1839. "Some of the Dakota women pack upon their backs burdens such as the men could not lift, so little accustomed are they to labour." Later that year she wrote to her mother after witnessing the distribution of turnips in the village. "Today if you had been here," she wrote, "you would have seen a specimen of Indian character—women busily engaged at work—men marching or sauntering about as if they were a superior race of beings . . . A great number went to the field, & you might have seen old & young women returning with nearly a bushel of turnips slung very carelessly or rather, dexterously, upon their backs while the young men came twirling one on their fingers or eating it as they stepped proudly by."[24]

What the missionaries understood to be begging was in fact the Dakota holding the Americans to their own standards of social propriety. Redistribution and generosity were central concepts in Dakota life. Rather than—as the missionaries understood it—squandering resources by supporting "the many sick & lazy, who are indefatigable beggars," redistribution occurred within a web of reciprocal obligation. When one family had plenty they shared it, knowing that in times of dearth, celebration, or remembrance their families and neighbors would share in return. When the missionaries did not insert themselves into this web of reciprocal redistribution, the Dakota proved adept at suggesting the inconsistencies of the missionary position. "When they, having nothing, are so liberal, they think strange that we who have, in their estimation, so many things, should withhold anything which they ask us for," wrote Mary Riggs in 1838. "And when we say the Bible says we should love our neighbors as we love ourselves, they ask why then do we not divide what we have with them, 'that would be loving them as well as ourselves.'" When persuasion would not work, the Dakota resorted to instruction by example. "We are obliged to pull our half grown turnips to secure any share for ourselves," mused Mary in 1841. "Our potatoes were taken in bushels."[25]

Similarly, while the missionaries understood farming to be a male enterprise, the Dakota disagreed. "Am I a woman that I should hoe corn[?]" asked one Dakota man when it was suggested he take up farming. "I thought I was a man." Farming was the work of women, just as hunting game was that of men—roles fundamental to Dakota social organization as ordained by the life-force of the universe. "If we should abandon the customs of our ancestors the Wakan would be angry with us and we would die," paraphrased Thomas Williamson on behalf of his Dakota informants. Williamson understood that no change in work roles could come about without change in religious belief. "From this we see that all efforts to civilize the Dakotas without giving them the gospel must prove entirely abortive," he wrote to David Greene in 1839.[26]

For the missionaries, this program of civilization was key: altering gender roles, and thereby altering marriages, would, along with Christian instruction, make the Dakota give up their existing living patterns. Given this interlocking set of beliefs, it is unsurprising to find that the missionaries considered those women who learned to knit and weave to present the greatest promise of conversion to Christianity and "civilized" life. "As you are ever interested in the advancement of these poor Indians towards civilization & Christianizing," wrote Mary Riggs to her mother in November 1839, "you will rejoice whenever progressive steps are taken . . . And surely in a country so inclement & among a people so poorly clad & so ignorant, a few yards of rude cloth, manufactured by Indian women, would at least be an encouraging omen. Last Thursday, the first piece made in the Sioux country was completed." Williamson also considered the moment one of great promise. "Many of the women are now desirous to learn to spin and weave . . . We feel that it is a great advance to have brought them to this," he wrote to David Greene. "It is greater than can be realized by any who are not acquainted with the strong prejudices connected with the religions of the Sioux and forbidding them to work as civilized people do it appears to me that nothing but the Spirit of God operating on their minds could have brought them to this."[27]

Yet despite this interpretation, the missionaries recorded no increase in the number of Dakota women attending church to correspond with the interest they showed in weaving cloth. Given the increasing scarcity of game across the region and the long hours of labor involved in working hides, it seems more plausible that Dakota women saw weaving, knitting, and sewing for what they were—an opportunity to replace dwindling resources. Calico and blankets had long been available through trade, but weaving on the missionaries' loom involved no cost or barter. There is also some evidence to suggest church attendance had little to do with belief in a Christian God. Mary's washerwoman, for example, was absent from church for two weeks after Mary had chastised her daughter. For Mary's wash help, church attendance was a means to earn the favor of the missionary family for whom she worked, while absence expressed anger in a manner she was sure they would notice.[28]

Even when the Dakota experimented with changes in gender-role behavior, these changes were not irrevocable or without larger social consequences. On March 28, 1839, Mary and Stephen Riggs accepted Anpetnakitoninwien, a young Dakota girl, into their household. Anpetnakitoninwien became responsible for sweeping the schoolroom, and Mary began teaching her to knit, wash, and sew. Just over four months later Anpetnakitoninwien's father was part of a war party dispatched against the Ojibwe to avenge the death of several Dakota families at Ojibwe hands the previous year. Stephen Riggs vehemently opposed the action and refused to grind corn for the young men to take on their journey. Refusing to aid such an endeavor placed Riggs at odds with the Dakota community. The war party shot two of the mission cows before leaving, and Anpetnakitoninwien was ordered home. In a separate incident, "a full blooded Sioux" man, Simon Anawangmani, was baptized in February 1841 and accepted into the church along with his wife and children. Simon won the approbation of the missionaries by helping them build a new church and beginning to farm. His wife, however, did not welcome the changes, and in the summer of 1842 moved her tipi to her mother's camp circle, leaving Simon behind. By farming, Simon had "made himself a woman" and was taunted and rejected by many of the Dakota at Lac qui Parle.[29]

Dakota polygamy greatly troubled the missionaries at Lac qui Parle, despite their own acknowledgment that the practice was rare. Within the framework of the American state, polygamy upset the economic and political exchange of services between husbands and wives that gave society its shape. More specifically, Thomas Williamson named the possibility of Dakota men taking several wives, often sisters, as one of the chief obstacles in "making the Dakotas a Christian people." Setting aside the fact that Dakota polygamy occurred most often when war left women without husbands and was therefore a means to absorb that loss, the missionaries remained stuck on the fact that polygamy was "inconsistent with the principle of the gospel." They were sensible of the fact that the practice was too rooted in Dakota culture to be undone without considerable problems: to insist that Dakota men "put . . . [their wives] away could cause us to be evil spoken of and perhaps deter any from listening to the truth," wrote Thomas Williamson to David Greene in 1837. There were also considerable theological problems to resolve. "And as respect the women. Who is to detirmine [sic] which of several is a man's wife. Is it less improper for one to continue to cohabit with a man who has another wife than for the man to have several wives[?] If we tell her to leave the man who chooses to dwell with her and claims her as his wife, how will we reconcile our advice with I Cor VII 13th[?]" Williamson asked his superiors. The Bible verse in question muddied the debate even further by being clear on only one issue: "And the woman which hath a husband that believeth not, and if he be pleased to dwell with her, let her not leave him."[30]

There was plenty of time to devote to such theological puzzles, as the missionaries could do little about polygamy—or anything else—except lament its existence to their superiors, colleagues, and families. For all their efforts, the missionaries effected little change in the lives of Dakota families in the early years of the station. In 1842, five years after the Riggses arrived in the Upper Midwest, Thomas Williamson estimated that the church at Lac qui Parle contained 42 members in good standing, that 132 adults and children had been baptized, and that an average of 45 students attended morning classes at the mission school—this from among a Dakota population that numbered in the thousands. Williamson's tally was not without qualification. On March 1, 1842, most of the Dakota "scattered off to their sugar camps," reducing school attendance to "[s]ome days none and others from 2 to 3 to 12 or 15. We cannot expect to have much if any school from this time till corn is ripe," he wrote, bearing witness to the persistence of Dakota seasonal practices and the gender and kinship roles which gave those practices shape. Further, he wrote, many of the children who attended school "have no wish to learn and never looking at a book except in the school room forget during the summer nearly all they have learned the previous winter . . . Many after having made considerable progress wander off & never return." Men, whose gendered work roles stood to change the most—to make them like women—if they adopted Western practices, stayed away from the church almost completely. This reflected, in Williamson's own words, "as much success [at the station] as in former years." The Dakota showed little interest in what the missionaries had to offer.[31]

Yet the presence of the missionaries did suggest that there were changes afoot in the region, and some of the weddings Mary witnessed in her first year of married life made that point. While the Dakota overwhelmingly resisted missionary influence and used missionary resources to their own ends, the altered marriage patterns of upper midwestern traders gave notice that the balance of power in the region had cautiously begun to shift. Trader marriages were the canaries in the mine, providing the first indication of the transformations yet to come.

Joseph Renville, whose fort had provided the focal point for trade in and around Lac qui Parle since 1823, was in many ways a quintessential fur trader from the Upper Midwest. Born in 1779, the son of a French trader and a Kaposia Dakota woman, Renville spent his formative years among his mother's relatives. Sent to Canada at age nine to be educated by a Catholic priest, Renville learned to speak (but not read) French and returned to the Upper Midwest around age eighteen to become a voyageur for British trader Robert Dickson. Sometime before 1797 Renville married a Dakota woman according to Dakota custom, and the two had eight children. Renville fought for the British in the War of 1812 and later worked as a Dakota translator for the U.S. government, yet his most consistent occupation was that of fur trader. In 1823 he established Fort Renville at Lac qui Parle, the trading post he would manage with the aid of his sons until his death in 1846.[32]

As a trader, Renville was a cultural mediator, offering counsel and hospitality to agents of the U.S. government, explorers, and missionaries from the East. Renville's support of the ABCFM mission at Lac qui Parle went a long way toward the Dakota's acceptance of the church in their midst, while his family made up the vast majority of the congregation every Sunday. Nevertheless, the trust placed in Renville by the Dakota (and their congruent willingness to trade with him) rested in large part upon his respect for and practice of Dakota culture as well as on his observation of kinship obligations. "His relatives among the Sioux are numerous, and this contributes not a little to expanding the great influence of his generous and liberal acts which come from his heart," observed French explorer Joseph Nicollet in 1838. Dakota was Renville's first language as well as that of his wife and children. His daughter's wedding in 1838 was celebrated at home with her Dakota family members rather than in the missionary's meetinghouse on top of the hill. When his eldest son died in 1839, Renville observed Dakota funerary practices, wrapping the body in white and scarlet cloth and holding a giveaway after the burial was complete—much to Mary Riggs's chagrin. For several weeks after his son's death, Renville stayed away from the mission church, turning to Dakota culture in his time of grief rather than to that of the missionaries and causing the latter to worry that their enterprise was doomed.[33]

Almost every trader in the region had taken a Native wife, such an alliance giving him access to a kin group that often extended over several villages and hundreds of miles. Hazen Mooers, who traded among the Dakota at Lac Traverse until the late 1830s, had a Dakota wife named Grey Cloud. Both Louis Provencalle (based at Traverse des Sioux) and Jean Baptiste Faribault (Lac Traverse and St. Peter's) had married Dakota women and traded with their bands. William Aitkin, trader at Fond du Lac, had taken an Ojibwe wife, while Joseph Rolette had married a Métis woman at Pembina. Such partnerships were standard practice in fur trade country and had been since the seventeenth century.[34]

Yet in one key respect, Renville's lifestyle differed from that of the fur traders around him—his marriage had been formalized by a Christian ceremony. Renville initially married his wife according to Dakota practice, "purchasing" her (in the misapplied words of biographer E. D. Neill) with gifts to her family. At some point after this initial ceremony, however, Renville and his wife traveled to Prairie du Chien to formalize their marriage in front of a Catholic priest.[35]

This practice might easily be explained by Renville's Catholicism if not for the fact that across the region other traders were solemnizing their marriages—previously solemnized "according to the custom of the country"—in a similar fashion. Philander Prescott, a trader near Fort Snelling and later at Traverse des Sioux, had married his Dakota wife, Nah-he-no-Wenah, sometime in the winter of 1823 to 1824. "I began to think about getting married after the Indian manner," he wrote in his memoir, "so I took ten blankets, one gun, and 5 gallons of whiskey and a horse and went to the old chief's lodge. I laid them down and told the old people my errand and went off home. The third day I received word that my gift had been accepted." In 1837, however, Prescott and Nah-he-no-Wenah were married in a Christian ceremony at the Lake Harriet mission church, with Stephen and Mary Riggs among their invited guests. Nah-he-no-Wenah, dressed in "moccasins, blue broadcloth pantalets & skirt with a fine calico short gown . . . several dozen strings of dark cut glass beads . . . ear drops [and a] blue broadcloth blanket thrown over her shoulders," seemed, to Mary Riggs, to feel "a little unpleasantly" about the ceremony. Joseph Brown, a later entrant into the fur trade business in the region, followed the practice of marrying women who could promote his success in the fur trade industry by their kinship ties. His first wife, Helen, was the Dakota daughter of Robert Dickson, a successful British fur trader; his second was Margaret McCoy, the Métis daughter of his chief voyageur; while his third wife, Susan Frénière, was one of Joseph Renville's Dakota step-nieces. Nevertheless, he never married according to "the custom of the country," preferring to solemnize his first marriage before a justice of the peace in Prairie du Chien, his second in a Christian ceremony presided over by Thomas Williamson, and his third before a justice of the peace in St. Paul.[36]

A central skill of any successful fur trader was an eye for opportunity, especially when it came to judging which alliances would

generate the most financial and political gain. Historically those judg-
ments had covered a wide range of possible actions; whether to run
whiskey past the watchful eyes at Fort Snelling; whether to side with
the Indian agent or a Native band; what credit to advance, at what
rate, and to whom. With the proliferation of missionaries across the
region, the increasing scarcity of game, and by 1836 the expansion
of Wisconsin into a fully fledged territory to the east, it would have
been clear to most traders that the old system was under threat and a
new social order was gathering in the wings. Solemnizing marriage
according to the standards of that new society while preserving kinship ties to the Native communities of the region allowed traders to
suggest their allegiance to both the old system and the new—depend-
ing on which would benefit them most—during a period of transition.
Their repositioning was astute. In Green Bay, Wisconsin, "custom"
marriages were one of the first things targeted by the U.S. courts
as untenable in an American state. Alliances with Native women
were judged permissible by the court, but only if they were solemnized according to American standards, thereby endowing husband
and wife with the legal identities so central to American social order.
Renville, Prescott, and Brown had positioned themselves to meet the
coming change.[37]

Marriage was a key life experience within each cultural group
that met at Lac qui Parle, providing the means for missionaries, traders, and the Dakota to honor specific sets of spiritual, economic, and
familial principles. Marriage provided structure to a person's day-to-
day responsibilities, governed how one individual related to another
in a variety of situations, and linked couples to a set of corporate beliefs about the ways in which society functioned best. Conflicts over
marriage reflected wider conflicts between those corporate systems

of belief. Yet in the face of those conflicts, little altered among the missionaries or the Dakota as they policed their own sense of marital propriety. That lack of change reflected the determination of both groups to hold fast to their traditions, even in a period of material uncertainty, as well as the failure of the missionaries to "transform the wilderness" as they had hoped. As the marital practices of select traders suggest, however, change was coming, requiring new allegiances to be established by the middlemen of the Upper Midwest. Marriage at Lac qui Parle was a tool of resistance, judgment, and adaptation, a barometer of cultural change.

For all Americans vested in the "civilizing" of the Upper Midwest, the maintenance of Euro-American family life was of singular importance, an active component of the social and cultural world they hoped to make. This was true not only for the missionaries scattered throughout the region but for the officers stationed at Fort Snelling, representatives of a young republic's western ambitions. Within a stone garrison, built atop a hill, with wide walls to demarcate the line between Native and American space, officers commanded households that, by their labor, produced status and society for those members of the infantry posted to the Upper Midwest. Slaves were integral members of those households, engaged in the productive work of making "civilization" while struggling to maintain households of their own. Such was the political nature of family life, performed at the behest of the American state.

Fort Snelling was built in Dakota country, high upon the bluffs above the Minnesota and Mississippi rivers.

꒰ ꒱

CHAPTER THREE

The Politics of the
Garrison Household

I{N 1845, FRANCES WEBSTER wrote a severely displeased letter
to her brother Edmund, a recent graduate of West Point Academy.
Frances came from a military family—her father had served in the
War of 1812 and risen to the rank of colonel by the time he resigned
his commission in 1821, while a second brother, Ephraim, began his
career in the infantry in 1826. Ephraim rose swiftly through the ranks
and served at posts across the United States' western front, including
Fort Snelling in 1837 and 1838. Frances herself married a military
man—Lucien Bonaparte Webster, an artillery officer—and by 1845
they had settled at Hannock Barracks in Maine. From there Frances
launched a blistering attack on Edmund when she heard he intended
to join the infantry, like his brother, rather than the artillery, like
his brother-in-law. "What possible advantage you imagine you can
obtain by going into the Infantry I cannot conceive," she wrote. "[A]ll
who have any knowledge of the subject and will give an unpreju-
diced opinion at once yield the superiority to the Artillery in point of
position and society while the emolument is the same." Frances had

very specific fears. "In the Infantry you must all your life be con-
fined to remote western frontier posts with little or no society beyond
your garrison," she wrote, "until you gradually assimilate to the demi-
civilized races who surround you."[1]

To join the U.S. Infantry was, without a doubt, to commit one-
self to service in locations far from mainstream American society:
Nathan Jarvis, surgeon at Fort Snelling from 1833 to 1835, called the
post a "retir'd & isolated spot." Jarvis was generally happy with his
post, and considered the rooms he occupied and the staff he had to
help him "a pretty large establishment" that was "abundantly supply'd."
The post possessed "glorious & every magnificent views, a serene &
delightful atmosphere & all that can ingratiate man with the works of
nature." This beauty helped, he believed, to "compensate in some manner for our seclusion in this distant region so far from the delights of
society and civilized life." The want of society at the fort was a
repeated theme in Jarvis's letters to his family. "One thing is only want-
ing that is society," he wrote his brother, as "our garrison constitutes
almost the only white population in the country." Left to their own
devices, he told his father in October 1833, the bachelor officers "are
very agreeable men although too much addicted to cards, which is the
prevailing vice in all the outposts where men are shut out from amusements during the long & severe winter." In a letter to his sister in 1834,
Jarvis suggested a solution. "Mary all I want now is a *wife*, can you pick
me out one?" he asked.[2]

A wife—a household—was central to the colonial venture at Fort
Snelling. Far from assimilating into nonwhite society, as Frances Webster supposed was the norm, the officers and their families at Fort
Snelling worked hard to maintain the trappings of a "civilized" life
while posted at their "retir'd and isolated spot." In the upper chambers

of the officers' quarters, wives and children, friends and guests worked and visited, dined and played. Their labor and leisure depended on other members of the household—the servants and slaves who toiled below stairs. This was key. Despite the fort's location in land above the 30° 36′ parallel—a marker that, after 1820, meant the region should have been free territory—slavery flourished at the post in support of the lifestyle white officers pursued. It was slavery and servitude that released officers' wives from the relentless domestic labor undertaken by almost all other married women in the region, and slavery and servitude that made the lifestyle of bachelor officers possible.

While slave labor supported white households, however, slaves had limited means to create households of their own. Across the United States, slavery was predicated in part upon the understanding that enslaved men and women, as chattel, lacked the legal capacity to enter into a marital contract and thereby enjoy legal protection over their family life. Yet the peculiarities of serving at Fort Snelling complicated this state of affairs. At least two enslaved individuals—Dred Scott and Harriet Robinson—entered into a marriage solemnized according to Euro-American legal rites at the fort, the ceremony presided over by Lawrence Taliaferro, local Indian agent and justice of the peace. Taliaferro considered it his duty to encourage marriage as a civilizing force in a region where Native marital practices overwhelmingly held sway.

Marriage was, when viewed from within the upper-story rooms of officers and their families, of central importance in determining social rank, sociability, and belonging; when viewed from below stairs, marriage could sometimes act as a claim of independence and agency among the enslaved. Yet perhaps the most important viewpoint in determining the particular intersection of marriage and slavery at

Fort Snelling was the gaze Euro-Americans presumed Native communities turned constantly toward the fort. It was beneath this gaze that they performed their marriages; it was in anticipation of this gaze that households were created and maintained.

❦

The gradations of "civilized life" at Fort Snelling were communicated by the physical space in which individuals lived, slept, and worked. That the inhabitants of the fort considered themselves distinct in purpose and lifestyle from those who lived outside it was apparent from the thick stone wall that surrounded the garrison by 1824—a defense against potential threats, but also a line of demarcation between American and Native space. The commanding officer of the fort lived in a two-story stone house which contained, in the words of Josiah Snelling, "in the first story two large rooms and two bedrooms, with a spacious hall in the centre; in the basement, a kitchen and offices"—room for the officer's family to receive visitors in spaces distinct from those reserved for work, and to sleep in spaces distinct from those they inhabited during waking hours. The commanding officer's quarters were detached from all other buildings close by, creating the greatest degree of privacy enjoyed by any inhabitant of the fort. The general officers' quarters, to the south of the commander's home, contained, "in the first story fourteen rooms with a small bed room annexed to each and in the basement a kitchen and pantry; six of these kitchens have cellars under the parade [ground]." Despite their adjoining status, the officers' barracks again afforded their inhabitants some privacy—a marked difference from the situation of enlisted men, who slept two to a bunk in a room with as many as eleven other men on the west side of the parade grounds. The enlisted men had basement amenities—their cooking and laundry were done in the cellars, where some married men were also quartered. Yet it was mostly servants and slaves who regularly spent time below stairs, a fact that gave spatial expression to their status as the lowest ranking inhabitants of the fort.[3]

The home of the commanding officer was designed to accommodate a family: it was anticipated that whoever was in charge of the garrison would be in charge of an extended household as well. The commanding officers ably filled the rooms allotted to them. Josiah Snelling and his wife, Abigail, were parents to six children while stationed at the fort, losing one, Elizabeth, in her infancy; Zachary Taylor and his wife, Margaret, arrived at the fort as parents of six. John Bliss was the father of one son while he commanded the garrison; Josiah and Elizabeth Plympton were parents of five; Seth Eastman and his wife, Mary, arrived at the fort as parents of three and welcomed two more children while at the post. These families were not simply private institutions—they were, on the bluff atop the junction of the Minnesota and Mississippi rivers, associative groups with a political identity. If the job of a fort and the inhabitants thereof was to begin the process of "civilizing" the far reaches of the West, then maintaining family ties, structured by coverture and all its attendant cultural responsibilities, was a key component of appropriating Native space for American purposes. The private relationships of the fort's elite were intended to be of public consequence to themselves, to their families and superiors in the East, and to the Native communities of the Upper Midwest.[4]

Members of the Fort Snelling community remembered this connection between "civilization" and family. In her memoirs, Charlotte Van Cleve, who spent her childhood at the fort, recounted her parents' reception of the news that they were to transfer from Connecticut to the Upper Midwest. Her father suggested that her mother stay behind, a bare fact upon which Charlotte elaborated with an imagined conversation between the two: "If my marriage vows mean anything, they mean that I am not to forsake you to such a time as this," Charlotte's mother told her father. "What would the comforts of this dear home, that the society of relatives and friends be to me, with you in a wild country, in the midst of a savage people, deprived of almost everything that makes life dear? No, no, my beloved; where thou goest I will go; thy people shall be my people; entreat me not to leave thee." Regardless of whether these were her mother's exact words, the sentiment behind them conveyed Charlotte's understanding of her parents' duty in the Upper Midwest—to be together as husband and wife in a land inhabited by "a savage people." John Bliss likewise linked the cause of "civilization" with his parents establishing a home at the fort in 1832. "A sight never to be forgotten was when on turning a point in the river there suddenly appeared, a mile or so before us, the imposing and beautiful white walls of Fort Snelling, holding, as though by main force, its position on a high precipitous bluff, and proudly floating the stripes and stars," he recalled. "It was a fortified oasis of civilization in a lovely desert of barbarism. We at one took possession of the commandant's quarters and were soon most comfortably established."[5]

As culturally designated guardians of the home, it was the job of the officers' wives to transform private and familial spaces into active realms of "civilized" life. These women were aware of the consequences of their actions, actively seeking to replicate in the West some version of the life they might have enjoyed in the East—this despite their isolation from that society, the difficulty of securing the material goods that supported their aspirations, and the lack of a wide set of peers to impress with their attempts. There was no widespread community—no town or city—of similarly positioned families to establish and police social norms. Instead the wives of officers policed their lifestyle for themselves in deference to the expectations in which they had been raised.

The work of creating an American home began before each family reached Fort Snelling. John Bliss, for example, remembered that his mother, on hearing of her husband's move to Fort Snelling, worked to make sure that "[b]edding and carpets were stowed away in water-tight tierces, and books in shallow boxes, so contrived that they could afterward be arranged in library form." Once in Cincinnati, she supervised the purchase of other supplies, including "hams, dried beef, tongues, rice, macaroni, family groceries in general, furniture, crockery, and what in these days would be considered a huge supply of wines and liquors." Ann Adams, a refugee from the failed Red River colony at the Canadian border who was employed by the Snellings, remembered "that Mrs. Major Plympton brought the first piano to [the] Fort."[6]

Once established in quarters, the officers' wives labored to create and maintain a vision of American life that befitted their husbands' rank. Many were not involved in relentless physical labor—their husbands' accounts with local traders suggest that, unlike their missionary counterparts, they bought soap, butter, candles, and socks rather than make them themselves. Married women did make clothes, however: Charlotte Van Cleve remembered watching "the nimble fingers of the officers' wives" as they made a wedding trousseau for Caroline Hamilton. Trader accounts also show numerous purchases of raw fabric—cotton, flannel, satinette, drab cloth, cambric, silk bombazette—as well as thread, buttons, ribbon, and animal skins for hats. The purchase of multiple skeins of silk may have been for dressmaking but might also have reflected that embroidery was a pastime at the fort: Ann Adams recalled that the officers' households "were attractive places, and showed evidence of style and good taste." At least some officers' wives had leisure time for reading and study—Charlotte Clark and Abigail Snelling studied French together under the tutelage of "a soldier named Simon" and later with the Italian Count Beltrami, who traveled through the Upper Midwest in 1823. John Bliss also recalled that the fort was equipped with "a good library."[7]

Offering hospitality by presiding over meals and games was a key responsibility of officers' wives. John Bliss remembered that "there was of course much sociability among the officers." More specifically, Ann Adams recalled that when "General [Winfield] Scott visited the Fort in 1826 . . . [he] was a guest of Colonel Snelling, and the spread was a creditable one. All the officers and their wives were present at his reception in full dress. Many of the ladies wore blazing diamonds." Nathan Jarvis recalled that on Christmas Eve 1834 the Bliss family entertained all the officers at the fort "with a splendid supper consisting among other delicacies of . . . venison, roast pig, sausages, mince & pumpkin pies, [and] new year cake." On Christmas Day Major Loomis and family welcomed everyone to a brunch at 10 AM, and in the evening there was supper at the sutler's house; "Music & Songs clos'd the amusements of the day." There was everyday hospitality, too—Captain Martin Scott was remembered by Charlotte Van Cleve as "a member of our family for many years," despite his bachelor status, perhaps in part owing to his "habit of asking my mother what and how much game she would like for the table and invariably bringing her just what she named."[8]

There is evidence that these patterns of hospitality had an impact on other Americans living outside the walls of the fort. Peter

Garrioch, an itinerant trader, laborer, and schoolmaster in the region, was a laboring member of missionary Jedediah Stevens's household at Lake Harriet in 1837. The missionary station was five miles from the fort and was among the limited "society" the garrison members could count upon. Garrioch, who considered the Upper Midwest to be a place of leveling opportunity, was appalled to be told by Stevens that he would need to sit and eat with the mixed-heritage and Indian employees of the mission station "in consequence of the smallness of ... [Stevens's] table, and from his frequently receiving visits of *ladies* and *gentlemen* from the Garrison." Not only would Garrioch be expected to eat with the Stevenses' "servants" but he would be served "after the *ladies* and *gentlemen!*" Garrioch complained that he would gladly have suffered through such a slight if he had "been treated thus in a civilized land, where it is necessary for every man to sustain his rank to a critical nicety." Garrioch did not believe the Midwest to be such a place—his greatest concern was that he had been told to eat with the "menial servants," who by their Indian background he considered to have "scarce ever taken a step from the state and condition in which nature left them." But Garrioch's experience reflected the fact that racial difference was not, alone, enough to structure the program of "civilization" in which the officers and their families were engaged; the observation and maintenance of social rank was an integral way in which officers and their families demonstrated and advanced the cause of "civilization" in the Upper Midwest. The officers' families at the fort were exacting in their observation of social niceties, while Stevens's own superiors in Boston had charged the missionary not only with preaching the gospel but also with demonstrating "the arts & comforts of civilized life."[9]

Under ideal circumstances, an officer's marriage created and maintained the social status of both husband and wife—but instances of impropriety could damage the standing of both. There were conventions to observe in courting and being wed, chief among them gaining the approval of a bride's parents for a given match—without it, a couple and their extended family might experience social isolation and shame. Jefferson Davis's courting of Knox Taylor was a case in point. Davis, who met Knox at Fort Crawford after her father's reassignment from Fort Snelling, was, according to John Bliss, roundly disliked by Zachary Taylor; "he did not like a single bone in his body," Bliss recalled. For certain, by 1835 the two had strongly disagreed over the proper administration of a court martial, and Taylor swore that Davis would not marry his daughter. Failing to gain Taylor's permission to marry, Davis and Knox eloped in 1835. "We all felt very bad about it," remembered John Bliss, "knowing what a blow it would be to the grand old colonel." Knox died in Mississippi later that same year without seeing her family again. Adultery was a similarly fraught issue. At Fort Snelling in 1838, Catherine Thompson "was seen by an unnamed officer entering [Lieutenant Harper] Tappen's quarters, in a cautious and suspicious manner," and when a party of officers went to investigate, they found Catherine hiding under Tappen's bed. The officers of the garrison prevented Catherine's husband, Lieutenant James Thompson, from injuring Tappen (or worse), but both Catherine and Tappen were considered by the fort's command to be unfit to remain at the garrison. Tappen was forced to resign his commission, and he and Catherine were sent downriver to St. Louis the very next day. In each instance the propriety attached to marriage had been broken, and officers and their families acted to reject such a breach.[10]

Such was the "civilizing" activity above stairs—but it was the activity in the cellars and basement kitchens that was most vital in the maintenance of social rank at the fort. Establishing a "civilized" society at the garrison depended on the purchase of labor—sometimes that of a free person, like Ann Adams, but most often that of an enslaved man or woman. The free labor pool around the fort was small, made up of refugees from Selkirk's Red River settlement and some family members of men connected with the fur trade; within the fort the wives of enlisted men worked as laundresses, servants, and hospital matrons. Shortages of labor were not uncommon, either for lack of any available help or help of a certain sort. When explorer George Featherstonhaugh visited the fort in 1835, he learned that "the commandant's lady had been for some time without a servant of any kind." Across the river, trader Henry Sibley hired two refugees from the Red River settlement to work in his home but found them unsatisfactory—too noisy, too dirty, leaving too much undone. His solution was to hire, in the words of scholar Lea VanderVelde, "a mulatto man, who he occasionally beat when he was displeased, to cook for him."[11]

Numerous slaves lived and worked at Fort Snelling in the pre-territorial period. In VanderVelde's estimation, Lawrence Taliaferro, the Indian agent whose home was located near the fort, "owned 21 slaves over the course of his life, but usually only six or seven at a time." Those slaves were sometimes loaned to officers within the garrison. In 1826, Colonel Snelling arranged to have Taliaferro's "Servant Boy William until the 1st of October next for this *Victuals & clothes*," while in 1829, Captain Plympton offered to buy Taliaferro's "Servant Girl Eliza." Taliaferro did not sell her, telling Plympton that "It was my intention to give her freedom after a limited time but that Mrs. P could keep her for two years or perhaps three." Other officers made their own arrangements. Sometime around 1827, Captain Day purchased James Thompson, a slave, from John Culbertson, sutler of the fort, before Day's redeployment to Fort Crawford; Thompson was then purchased and freed by Alfred Brunson, a Methodist minister. In 1833 Major Bliss and his family, en route to Fort Snelling from Pittsburgh, stopped in St. Louis to buy groceries and "the last of our necessary purchases . . . to wit: a nice-looking yellow girl and an uncommonly black man." In 1835 Lieutenant Storer arrived at the fort with a new bride and Betsy, his family's slave; in 1836 Dr. John Emerson arrived to take up a position as post surgeon and brought along his slave, Etheldred Scott. By 1838 there were twelve nonwhite "servants" working at the fort, of which three were definitely slaves. There is evidence that designating all laborers at the fort as "servants" was a genteel artifice. Lawrence Taliaferro freely admitted that he kept slaves during his tenure in the Upper Midwest, but his journals were more likely to reference such men and women as "servants" or "that negro," while John Bliss remembered the purchase of his family's slaves in St. Louis but often fell to calling them servants in his memoirs. The documentation used by the U.S. Army to pay officers for their hired help also supported this linguistic turn: officers could make claims "For _____ private Servants," leaving historians to guess as to the status of laborers with dark or black skin, brown or black eyes, and black or dark hair.[12]

The officers at Fort Snelling came from a culture in which slavery flourished and which supplied them with multiple models for the use of slave labor. In the antebellum United States, few slaves lived on sprawling plantations; most lived and worked on small farms raising cotton, rice, sugar, tobacco, and crops for family use. Not all enslaved men and women worked in fields, however. Many rural slave-owners used slave labor in their homes, where women worked as housekeepers, cooks, nursery maids, and laundresses and men were employed as blacksmiths, wheelwrights, valets, and stable hands. A sizeable number of slaves also worked in urban communities, hiring themselves out for a fee which was returned, in whole or part, to their owner. Men could work in construction, in skilled trades such as carpentry, at railroad terminals, and on docks. Women had more limited options, the most skilled profession open to them being midwifery, their more usual occupations including dressmaking, laundry, and market work.[13]

The work undertaken by enslaved men and women at Fort Snelling was rarely, if ever, described by those who witnessed it, yet there are distinct clues to the type of labor enslaved men and women performed. It is highly unlikely, for example, that any of the slaves brought to Fort Snelling were field hands. What agricultural cultivation existed at the fort was for subsistence purposes and was one of the responsibilities of the enlisted men, who raised crops of corn, potatoes, and wheat. While officers' families had their own gardens, those plots were not large enough to warrant full-time labor by an enslaved man or woman. Transforming raw foodstuffs into the dinners enjoyed above stairs, however, did require the labor of the enslaved, particularly women. Fires had to be constantly tended; salt meat soaked and boiled or stewed; fowl scalded, plucked, and roasted; bread baked weekly; pies and puddings set above an open fire. Vegetables were boiled and pickled and stored; corn dried and milled and baked into cakes; fish were gutted, fillets grilled; pans were scalded after each meal. In addition, clothes were sewn, laundered, and mended; mistresses dressed; bedclothes washed and aired; rooms swept, rugs beaten, dressers and cabinets kept free of dust. All this took place without an interior staircase between the upper and lower floors of the house—meals, laundry, dishes, chamber pots, brooms, and dustrags had to be moved between floors by the exterior stairs, which baked in the summer and froze in winter's depths.[14]

Enslaved men had other occupations, including working as valets and stable hands. William took care of Josiah Snelling's clothes and served him food; Dred Scott had experience working as a valet for four officers at Fort Armstrong before doing the same for Dr. Emerson at Fort Snelling. It seems likely that the Bliss family's male slave, Hannibal, shouldered some responsibilities as a valet, with Bliss recalling that even in later years, Hannibal (by then free) visited him at college and "put my belongings in order, and polished my shoes." Captain Scott, who was stationed at the fort from 1821 until approximately 1840, kept a "negro servant" to take care of his horses and his large pack of hunting dogs. In order to demonstrate his marksmanship, Scott also required his "servant" to stand with an apple on his head, through which Scott would "send a ball." In all of these instances, enslaved men and women's labor secured the prestige of officers and their families alike.[15]

What evidence we have about slave life at Fort Snelling suggests that the isolation of the fort offered a handful of slaves some slight freedoms. Most work undertaken by slaves was done in close quarters with those who owned their labor; even work with horses and dogs could not have been done far from an officer's quarters, considering the fort's limited space. Yet slaves did have some control over their movement and time. Hannibal, the male Bliss family slave, was twice caught selling spruce beer to the enlisted men—beer he had brewed himself. The fact that he was able to conceal his brewing activities, particularly after being caught once, suggests that some slaves were not closely watched and had time to call their own. Beyond the time required for Hannibal to distill his ale, he must also have possessed enough freedom of movement to leave the garrison to collect spruce bark—a task that was not easy by the 1830s, when most of the local environment had been deforested to provide the fort with construction materials and fuel.[16]

The disappearance of one of the Taylor family's slaves from Fort Crawford in the summer of 1835 also suggests the freedom of movement some slaves may have possessed. That summer, Major John Bliss, commanding officer at Fort Snelling, received a letter from his friend and colleague Colonel Zachary Taylor, now the commanding officer at Fort Crawford in Prairie du Chien. There was a disturbance in the household: one of Taylor's "female slaves had most mysteriously disappeared, leaving not a trace or clue behind," recalled Bliss's son, John. "No sooner had my father mentioned it, than up I spoke and said, 'why she is at _____' (mentioning a place I have since forgotten)." Bliss the elder was flabbergasted and asked his son how he knew such a thing: "'Well,' said I, 'when we were at the Colonel's, she asked me one day if I could write. I answered that I could. She then asked if I would write a letter to her husband for her, to which I at once assented, and wrote down the words as she gave them, and among other things, she said she would see him next month, by fair means or foul.'"

A discussion of Bliss the younger's failure to tell an adult about the exchange ensued ("'Why didn't you report it at once?' asked my father. 'Well,' I replied, . . . 'I doubt if it would have been just the thing for me to have betrayed her confidence.'") Luckily for father and son, the next month's mail brought reassuring news: "Mrs Taylor was almost paralyzed one day when the girl quietly stepped into the kitchen and set about her duties as though nothing had happened; she had performed the precise journey that her letter indicated." This

enslaved woman's experience implies an almost lackadaisical attitude among military personnel about limiting slave movement in the
Upper Midwest. There is no evidence that Taylor's letter to Bliss
asked for assistance in tracking the woman, and none that on hearing where the woman had gone Bliss sent troops to find her, nor word
to Taylor about the younger Bliss's confession so that Taylor might
do so if he chose. In comparison, various commanding officers at
Fort Snelling did spare manpower to pursue and bring back enlisted
men who had deserted. While such an act might suggest the greater
value of enlisted men than slaves to the fort, such men were usually
drummed out of the company, suggesting that the point was one of
honor or military responsibility rather than an indication of a soldier's worth.[17]

What little we know about the disappearance of the Taylor family's
slave suggests that she felt comfortable both leaving Fort Crawford
and returning again. Certainly her request that a commanding officer's son write a letter to her husband about her visit does not suggest she had any particular fear about being pursued by the military.
While we know almost nothing about the extenuating circumstances
of her disappearance—her destination, for example, or whether her
skin color was light enough to allow her to blend in to other communities—it is not hard to imagine the difficulties Americans faced
in closely policing the movement of slaves. Isolated from a larger
slaveholding culture, slaveholders in the Upper Midwest had little to
no support in restricting the world in which slaves lived. Beyond the
walls of Fort Snelling, for example, lived Dakota people who within
their culture had no concept of slavery or of human beings as chattel
property. Isolation both made and unmade slavery in the region. It
was isolation from settled American society that made slave labor

attractive to many officers and families at the fort: an absence of local American communities meant domestic servants and laborers were few and far between in the Upper Midwest. Such isolation, however, also lent itself to making slavery in the region an idiosyncratic and individualized experience.

The disappearance of the Taylor family's slave also demonstrated the resiliency of enslaved men and women in maintaining and perpetuating family ties despite separation. Such resiliency was a national phenomenon, a necessary response to separations inflicted upon enslaved men, women, and children by forced sale, disparate work locales, and a lack of legal redress. The Taylor case might also point to another unusual dimension of slavery in the Upper Midwest: the existence of formal marriages between slaves. Sometime between May 8, 1836, and September 14, 1837, Harriet Robinson, a slave owned by Lawrence Taliaferro, was married in a civil ceremony to Dred Scott, a slave owned by Fort Snelling post surgeon John Emerson. The ceremony was given particular resonance by Taliaferro's role as officiant—the Indian agent was the local justice of the peace, a recognized legal representative of the state, and an advocate of Euro-American marriage as a tool by which civilization might take root in the region. "Having the authority of a justice of the Peace I deem it a more ritcheous [sic] course to give some solemn form to these proceedings and marry those disposed to be firmly as man & wife," he wrote in his journal in 1835, "rather than see an indiscrimite [sic] intercourse—or a want of proper respect for the married state or the sex."[18]

As Indian agent, Taliaferro spent as much of his time among traders and American Indian communities as he did with the inhabitants of the fort. As such, he was surrounded by individuals who did not show "proper respect" for Euro-American marriage; indeed, he himself had entered into a custom of the country marriage with Dakota woman Anpetu Inajinwin in the 1820s, resulting in the birth of a daughter, Mary, in 1828. By 1835 his nearest neighbors were Henry Sibley, who would enter into a custom marriage with Red Blanket Woman by the winter of 1839–40, and Jean Baptiste and Pelagie Faribault, who never married according to Euro-American law. Daniel Lamont, who married Hanyetukihnayewn; Martin McLeod, who married Mary Elizabeth Ortley, an Anglo-Dakota woman; Philander Prescott, who married Nah-he-no-Wenah; and Benjamin Baker, whose wife was Ojibwe, were among the traders who lived and worked in the vicinity. Everywhere outside of the fort, custom of the country marriages flourished. This ultimately proved personally and professionally insupportable to Taliaferro. At the same time that Anpetu Inajinwin was pregnant with his child, Taliaferro was back East, marrying Elizabeth Dillon, the daughter of a Bedford, Pennsylvania, innkeeper. On their return to the Upper Midwest, the Taliaferros set up their household as a model of civilized living and engaged in much the same activities as the officers and their wives at the fort: visiting, entertaining, providing hospitality, and outfitting their home with the material goods that marked their household as respectably American. Taliaferro not only entered into a Euro-American marriage but officiated at the marriages of others and recorded that fact in his autobiography with genuine pleasure. Oliver Cratte was married to a Miss Graham; James Wells to another Miss Graham (sister of the first); Alpheus R. French to Mary Henry; and "Dred Scott with Harriet Robinson, my servant girl, which I gave him." The Scott's marriage was, like others, part of Taliaferro's commitment to enforcing "morality, as far as practicable" in the Upper Midwest.[19]

Yet throughout the slaveholding South, marriage between slaves was prohibited on the grounds that slaves, as property, possessed no autonomy and therefore no ability to contract with another person: a man whose body was owned by another could not become the head of a household under the strictures of coverture. Enslaved men and women instead formalized their marriages through community celebrations and ceremonies such as "jumping the broom," but these arrangements had no legal standing. John Bliss's reference to the "husband" of the Taylors' slave may simply have been a slip of the tongue, and we do not know whether her husband was enslaved or free. The Scotts' marriage, however, presided over by a justice of the peace, ran headfirst into the contradictions of a program of "civilization" that depended on marriage and slavery both.[20]

Property was central to the way in which Americans organized their thoughts regarding issues of race, culture, and governance in the nineteenth century. For most of the antebellum period, married women could not own property, differentiating them from their husbands, who could. While slavery lasted, the vast majority of black men, women, and children in the United States were considered the property of others—marriage and the legal protection of family were denied them. No matter their own definitions of kinship and responsibility, slaves were considered the legal dependents of white men, the latter's governance of slaves informing their civic authority to govern at large. Free black men and women were also severely limited in their engagement with civil society by black codes—laws that limited their personal liberty by reference to the skin color they shared with the enslaved. Such laws forged unity among white men of different economic fortunes at the expense of others, identifying governance as a white preserve.[21]

But Fort Snelling was isolated. What slavery could and should mean in the region was, in some small but meaningful sense, negotiable. Philosophies of governance were as powerful a force in the Fort Snelling community as elsewhere in the United States—they structured the actions of a community of officers and their wives who maintained their allegiance to codes of familial behavior not shared by the thousands of upper midwestern inhabitants around them. Yet philosophy could not conquer the realities of physical isolation. Officers wished for the comforts of a "civilized" life—a life that required the presence of domestic help in the household despite the dearth of free labor in the vicinity of the fort. Such wants pulled slavery into the Upper Midwest regardless of that territory's status as free. Isolation then shaped that experience of slavery, the rivers and woods of the Upper Midwest giving at least one enslaved woman the opportunity to steal away from her owners to see her husband and Hannibal the opportunity to make his illicitly brewed beer. The purpose of the fort's presence in that isolation—to act as the advance guard for the structures of the American state; to transform what Euro-Americans believed to be a wilderness—gave slavery its further peculiar character, convincing Indian agent and justice of the peace Lawrence Taliaferro to solemnize the marriage of Harriet and Dred according to the principles of Euro-American marriage that he hoped the Dakota, Ojibwe, and mixed-heritage inhabitants of the region would one day adopt.

That the Scotts were married is usually a footnote in a larger story. In 1846 Dred Scott filed suit for his freedom in St. Louis, claiming that his residence in the free territory of the Upper Midwest had manumitted his status. Harriet's own claim to freedom was subsumed within Dred's, despite the possibility that Taliaferro had freed her at the same time that he had seen her married, a claim the Indian agent made later in life and which scholars Lea VanderVelde and Sandhya Subramanian find consistent with Taliaferro's overall approach to manumitting his slaves during his lifetime. Any claim Harriet had to being free was never recorded or examined by the courts. The Supreme Court of the United States ruled on the Scott case in 1857, adjudicating that Congress had no constitutional right to prohibit slavery in the free territories; that as a slave Scott was not a citizen of the United States and therefore could not claim the protection of its court system; and that the Missouri Compromise had abrogated the Fifth Amendment rights of slaveholders and was therefore unconstitutional. For the Scotts, the most immediate consequence of the decision was that they remained enslaved. For slaveholders in the Midwest, the decision retroactively made the preterritorial practice of slavery at Fort Snelling constitutional. For the country, the decision added more fuel to the ongoing sectional disputes that would boil up into civil war.[22]

Yet Harriet and Dred's marriage was more than the basis for their joint suit for freedom—in the moment it occurred it encapsulated a set of truths about marriage at Fort Snelling that are easily overlooked. Marriage at the fort represented many often contradictory things: a relationship governed by individual lusts and wants; a means to claim social sanction and propriety; an attempt to create America in a non-American place; and a locus of resistance against social, philosophical, and legal norms. "Mary all I want now is a *wife*, can you pick me out one?" asked Nathan Jarvis of his sister in 1835. Such a want was a complicated thing within the garrison's walls.[23]

To marry was complicated—but so, in Euro-American society, was divorce. In a republic that linked marital and civic responsibility, divorce was a jealously guarded marital exit, available under limited circumstances to innocent parties wronged by their husband or wife. Where marriages broke down, so might social order, and it behooved legislators and the judiciary to shore up marital responsibilities, despite the potential personal cost to those involved. Sometimes, however, the breakdown of social order lurking behind a plea for divorce was so total that marital law could offer nothing in response. Such was the case of Joseph Brown and Margaret McCoy at the western fringes of Wisconsin Territory in 1840; in their divorce lurked a tale of instability bigger than one husband and his wife.

There are no surviving images of Margaret McCoy. Photographs of her female descendents—such as daughter Margaret, above—are the closest we can come to imagining how she looked.

CHAPTER FOUR

Margaret McCoy's Divorce

O N JANUARY 11, 1840, the Wisconsin territorial legislature passed An Act for the Relief of Joseph R. Brown, divorcing Brown from his second wife, Margaret McCoy. (Joseph had divorced his first wife in 1832.) Joseph and Margaret claimed residency in Crawford County, a vast region on the territory's western border that hugged the eastern shore of the Mississippi River past Fort Snelling and north. The legislature stipulated that the parties could divorce if they jointly wrote a separation agreement to be submitted to the Crawford County justice of the peace, dissolving their marriage as if it had never existed, and freeing Joseph and Margaret to marry again. Joseph was directed to provide Margaret with her "widow's thirds" (one-third of his property, both real and personal) as if he had died, and the legislature stipulated that the pair's children would remain legitimate even after the divorce. Joseph and Margaret signed their deed of separation—he with his name, she with her mark— on February 5, 1840; on August 11 the deed was certified by the chief justice of the supreme court of the territory, and at 5:00 PM on

April 29, 1841, the deed was "received, certified, and recorded" by the Crawford County registrar of deeds. In the deed, Joseph committed himself to provide for the economic support and education of his children and gave Margaret "two Calves, one Bay Mare, two breeding sows, a dozen Dung-hill fowl . . . improvements made . . . on a claim on the Red Rock Prairie, and three hundred and seventy-five dollars in specie" as her dower.[1]

Behind these words was an exceedingly complex story. According to the original petition for divorce submitted to the Wisconsin territorial legislature, Joseph had "been from a boy a resident within the Sioux Territory, and for many years past, a trader among said tribe." Margaret was "a half blood Chippeway . . . [who had] lived among the tribe until within a few years when the Peace that then existed between the tribes induced her father to locate himself near Fort Snelling." The two were married by missionary Thomas Williamson at Fort Snelling in 1836 but, according to the petition, were prevented from establishing a household together by "war, with all its sorrow, [that] had broken out between the Sioux of Lac Travers and the Chippeways of Red Lake." Hostilities "rendered it out of the question that one of Chippeway blood could venture unto [Dakota] country," yet Joseph was under contract to the American Fur Company: "arrangements . . . compelled him to proceed to Lac Travers, where he was detained until July 1838, during all which time the war continued between the two nations." More bands of the Dakota and Ojibwe joined the fight in 1839, leading the Browns to conclude that "the war now raging the whole extent of the two nations, precludes the possibility of your Petitioners being able to reside together, unless they should leave the vicinity of both tribes." Margaret, they argued, would be uncomfortable in a white settlement, "where the manners and customs were not familiar to her," especially since she was "unable to speak the English language," while Joseph argued that he was "incapable of any business other than the one he now follows" and that giving up the trade would make him "guilty of a breach of faith." There was no way forward, argued the Browns, save divorce. While "under present circumstances it is impossible we should be together," they wrote, they hoped the legislature would permit them to avoid becoming "a burden to each other, should either of us be inclined to form other matrimonial connection."[2]

Much of this public story of the Browns' married life was true. Joseph's presentation of himself as a Dakota trader in a time of immense regional upheaval was truthful; so was his brief description of Margaret's ancestry and migration in the region. Margaret's father, Francis McCoy, was an emigrant from Selkirk's Red River settlement, one of many who preferred to establish a home among the community of refugees and traders around Fort Snelling rather than remain on the agriculturally inhospitable high prairie. McCoy worked for Brown's trading operation and was foreman of that venture when Joseph and Margaret met. Margaret's mother is generally accepted to have had Ojibwe heritage. Joseph Brown's biographers suggest she may have been a Cadotte, a member of a powerful mixed Ojibwe and French trading family from Lake Superior. Records from Margaret's second marriage, however, suggest that her mother's maiden name was Lagrue, a name meaning "crane" in French, possibly signifying her connection to that Ojibwe clan. It was also true that the general shape of Joseph and Margaret's marriage followed the patterns of coexistence intrinsic to the fur trade, where non-Native men married Native women to gain a foothold in the enterprise. Given that general context, the divorce petition provided, at first glance, a familiar story with a tragic twist: a non-Native man entered the fur trade and took a Native wife to facilitate his business relationships, yet (despite years of such arrangements working well for Native communities and non-Native traders alike) war made this an untenable match.[3]

Such a tale required legislators to be persuaded by the broad strokes of the story and not to examine the situation too closely—not to ask why a Dakota trader would take an Ojibwe wife, not to ponder what advantage either could derive from such a relationship as it was traditionally defined. The real story of the Browns' marriage was much messier than the petitioners would have had legislators believe. We know that Joseph and Margaret's relationship began before 1836—their first child, Margaret, was born on November 14, 1835. In 1836, Joseph's uncle died in Pennsylvania, leaving money in trust for Joseph's legitimate heirs, and this prompted the couple to marry—a turn of events that Joseph admitted he had never anticipated. "When I arrived at St Peters, if anyone had told me I would marry that girl I should have thought them out of their minds," he wrote to his friend Henry Sibley in October 1836. Joseph was fifteen years old when he reached the Upper Midwest in 1820, and perhaps he meant to suggest that marriage had been an unfathomable object at the time. Perhaps, too, the Joseph of the 1830s, like his friend Sibley, future governor of Minnesota Territory, considered relationships with women of mixed-cultural or strongly Native backgrounds to be a stopgap on the way to a more "respectable" relationship. (Sibley fathered a child, born in 1841, with Red Blanket Woman, a member of Black Dog's band of the Mdewakanton; he married Sarah Jane Steele, an emigrant from Baltimore, in a Euro-American ceremony at Fort Snelling in 1843.)[4]

There is, of course, the strong possibility that Joseph spoke with feeling, that his relationship with Margaret had run its course or was never meant to be long term. In the same 1836 letter in which Brown remarked on the surprising nature of his marriage, he told Sibley that Margaret had agreed to "give me opportunity of getting a divorce before I will be *able* to marry, & then if necessary it is only the expense of a lawsuit and things will be *straight*." Neither Joseph nor Margaret considered divorce to be a necessary prerequisite for beginning a new relationship, however. Brown courted Susan Frénière, a Dakota woman from Lac qui Parle, who bore him a child at Lake Traverse in 1836; though the two would live together for the rest of their lives, they did not enter into a formal, Euro-American marriage until 1850. We also know, by the crudest of measures, that Joseph and Margaret continued their sexual relationship well after 1836: Margaret bore Joseph a second child, Mary, in 1838. Margaret also entered into other relationships during the duration of her marriage to Brown—she was four months pregnant with Peter Bouché's daughter when she and Joseph signed their deed of separation in 1841. By the end of that year she was married to Joseph Bourcier, a man who had worked for several years for Joseph Brown, and it was Bourcier with whom she would spend the rest of her life.[5]

Almost nothing from the legislative deliberations on the matter of the Browns' divorce survives. The records of the judiciary committees of both houses have been lost. There is no tally of votes from the council—the territory's upper house—showing the margin of legislators in favor of the divorce, much less their names. There are few consistencies in the biographies of the fourteen members of the lower house who voted in favor of the marriage's dissolution. Those who voted in favor of the divorce were slightly more likely to have established homes in the region before the territory was founded: six in favor, three opposed. Most were not heads of household at the founding of the territory—eight of those who voted yes were new emigrants, as were seven of those who voted no. Whatever personal relationships may have shaped the legislators' response to the petition are likewise lost. It seems certain that Brown was in Madison during the deliberations on his petition and could not have helped but meet members of the legislature given the cramped lodging situation in the town, yet the final divorce bill cost him handsomely in property and specie—what favor he may have met in having his bill brought before the council and house did not extend to the settlement to which he was forced to submit.[6]

There are other questions about the Browns' divorce which we may never be able to answer. What little we know about Margaret McCoy, for example, is gleaned from shards of information scattered through the papers of other midwesterners, Margaret's own illiteracy limiting the information she could record. We may never be able to piece together her motivations for marrying Joseph Brown or to understand why she waited three years to grant him the divorce he believed he could obtain on a whim. Beyond these circumstances, there is the question of her sense of self, the cultural identity she practiced and claimed, and the impact that had upon her choices throughout her life—important considerations that are, nevertheless, difficult to pin down.

Given this, it is tempting to dismiss the Browns' divorce as fascinating trivia—yet to do so is to miss the greater import of this single event. For all the unanswered questions surrounding Joseph and Margaret's divorce, the dissolution of their marriage provides us with an unparalleled window into the messy business of state making on the United States' western fringe. From the Browns' divorce we learn that being a legislator in Wisconsin Territory was an often unglamorous, farcical enterprise; that legislating marital dissolution was one way in which legislators sought to impose Euro-American social control on a region that defied it; that despite material hardships, the signing of treaties, and the slow pressure of increased Euro-American settlement in the region, this was an Ojibwe and Dakota place whose inhabitants were engaged in resistance to the plans of traders, government officials, and missionaries alike. Exactly why Joseph and Margaret were permitted to divorce may remain a mystery, but the stories that surround their divorce reveal much about a region in flux.

The very mechanism by which Joseph and Margaret's divorce was made public—the printed word, in the form of a statute neatly bound and published in 1840—suggests stability and orderliness, a claim, gilded with hindsight, for the inviolability of law. In its printed form the statute provides no context for its existence—the personal stories, upheavals, and day-to-day business of the men who voted for its passage fall away, leaving only their final deliberations. It is easy, then, to presume order when looking at the statute, to read back into the Madison of 1838 and 1839 a settled aspect that did not exist. Madison was founded on land owned by Judge James Doty in 1837. George Stoner, who arrived that year as a child, described the settlement as "a forest of giant oaks, among which were nested two or three log cabins, where the weary traveler was sheltered, fed and kindly cared for." Construction on the territorial capital began that year, but by 1838 little had been completed, and the first Madison-based legislators for the territory met in an unfinished, roughed-out building that fall. Ebenezer Childs recalled that the "floors were laid with green oak boards, full of ice; the walls of the room were iced over; green oak seats, and desks made of rough boards; [while] one fire-place and one small stove [heated the space.]" Finished space was at such a premium in the settlement that James Morrison housed his pigs in the basement of the capitol. During the session in which the legislators considered the Browns' divorce, Childs recalled, he would, when speakers became "too tedious . . . take a long pole, go at the hogs, and stir them up; when they would raise a young pandemonium for noise and confusion. The speaker's voice would become completely drowned, and he would be compelled to stop, not however, without giving his squealing disturbers a sample of his swearing ability."

Things were scarcely more refined when the legislators departed at the close of business each night. J. G. Knapp recalled that in 1838 a man seeking lodging in the town was lucky to find "two feet by six of floor . . . at two pence a square foot, where the weary passenger might spread his own blanket . . . and rejoice that he had so good a bed." By the time the legislature was in session, sleeping space was at even more of a premium, a situation relieved only by the fact that, in Knapp's words, men were "remarkably accommodating in those early times, and . . . could occupy a field bed, where they were forced to lie spoon fashion [with one another]. A frontier life is a mighty leveler; much like poverty, making men acquainted with strange bed fellows." The life of a legislator was far from grand. "The weather was cold," Childs recalled, "[and] the halls were cold, our ink would freeze, everything froze—so when we could stand it no longer, we passed a joint resolution to adjourn for twenty days. I was appointed by the two houses to procure carpeting for both halls during the recess; I bought all I could find in the Territory, and brought it to Madison, and put it down after covering the floor with a thick coating of hay."[7]

It was amid these circumstances that Wisconsin's territorial legislators sought to organize their thoughts about divorce. Such work was not unusual for legislators of the era—mechanisms for divorce had existed within the Anglo-American legal system from the earliest years of colonial settlement and by 1840 were in force in every state and territory but South Carolina. In 1839 the legislators of Wisconsin Territory—which had inherited its existing divorce laws from the territory of Michigan—passed An Act Concerning Divorce, transferring jurisdiction for divorce proceedings from the legislature to the judiciary. The act allowed for divorce in proven cases of adultery or impotence, while the grounds for legal separation—divorce *a mensa et thoro*—were expanded to include extreme cruelty, desertion, abandonment, or drunkenness. Legal separations did not undo the marriage contract, but modified it, removing individuals from the economic responsibilities required of them by coverture. A woman who won legal separation from her husband was generally owed his financial support but was excused from sharing or maintaining his home; men who won their case were generally excused from making financial provision for their wives.[8]

Such laws reflected a national trend—not toward impossibly fragile marriages but toward legislators exerting control over the way in which marriages ended. Americans had long sought exits from their marriages for many and varied reasons—because partners could not stand one another; because of abandonment, poverty, or a husband's disinterest in providing for his wife; because work was more easily found in another place; because of illness, incest, or abuse. But the law did not recognize such impediments as cause to dissolve a marriage contract—indeed, divorce was more closely aligned with criminal law than with the laws that allowed couples to wed. Divorce was a remedy offered to innocent parties who had been wronged—those who were chaste and blameless while their partners cheated; those who entered the marriage contract in full faith, unaware their partners were already married elsewhere; one who, in a woman's case, thought the marriage would produce children but found herself yoked to a man who could not consummate the marital act. For lack of a blameless victim and identifiable culprit—perhaps both parties cheated; perhaps the couple had sex but the wife's infertility invisibly prevented conception; perhaps everyone knew the parties hated one another and had fabricated a story to put their misery to an end—many an unhappy man and woman remained legally bound. In response, couples wrote their own deeds of separation or simply parted. These remedies were extralegal and pervasive, and in a country that so closely aligned the practical, philosophical, and legal responsibilities of marriage with the orderly political functioning of government, they threatened the ability of legislatures and judicial bodies to enforce a social order that best served the state. Expanding the reach of legal divorce put legislators and judges in charge of the process; it carefully and deliberately set the state in opposition to extralegal separation.[9]

Not all marital difficulties between Wisconsin couples, however, could be addressed by the 1839 law. Where complainants understood that their cases did not meet the standard set by the courts but felt there was merit in their petition, they approached the legislature for special redress. It is in those petitions that we find particular evidence of marital and social instability. Legislators proved consistent in their responses to such petitions—when faced with the stories of separated and unhappy couples whose troubles merely suggested that marriage could be miserable, they held firm: unhappiness, cruelty, and even abandonment were not sufficient cause for them to grant a couple a complete divorce. Samuel Hubbard of Platteville left his wife, Achesah, and moved to Wisconsin in 1836 because he had been "treated ... in a cruel and unbecoming manner, both by [her] words and actions." Achesah, Hubbard charged, had threatened his life, wounded him "with unlawful and deadly weapons ... [and] often told him that their youngest child belonged to another man." Sarah Leach of Green Bay was married on June 4, 1837, only to have her husband abandon her within two weeks. Hariet Tyrer claimed that she had married at the age of thirteen under false pretenses, having been led "to believe by the representatives of ... William Tyrer that he was a man of considerable property and of industrious habits." Not only did William turn out to be "destitute," "indolent," and "harsh," but Hariet claimed he was "of a suspicious and exceedingly jealous disposition." Rebecca Farrington, married in 1827 to "Alexander C. Farrington, then a man whose moral character stood high in the county of Oneida in the state of New York," experienced a rude awakening two years later when her husband was imprisoned for fraud in Vermont. Farrington escaped, traveled to Ohio, committed further frauds, was imprisoned, and had at some point in between "engaged in keeping a house of illfame in the city of New York under an assumed name." All of these petitions, and others like them, were denied—legislators rejected the idea that the rules of coverture, and therefore social order, should be suspended in any of these cases.[10]

Aside from the Browns, the only other successful petitioners for a legislative divorce between 1839 (when divorce was made a judicial responsibility) and 1841 (when the Browns' divorce was finalized) were Peter Howard of Mineral Point and Josiah Moore of Vernon. Peter's case was uncomplicated—his wife had engaged in "repeated and long continued acts of inconstancy and adultery," established grounds for divorce in the courts. His need for a legislative divorce rested on the fact that his wife lived in Tennessee and therefore was not available to participate in the proceedings—the matter was swiftly handled. Josiah Moore's case, however, was more complex: he had married Levisa Nichols in Oxford, Massachusetts, in 1827, but by 1831 she was insane. With the blessing of her family, Josiah emigrated to Wisconsin alone and began "improvement[s]" on 220 acres of land. Returning to Oxford in 1840 and finding his wife's condition unchanged, Josiah entered into a separation agreement with his wife's father, David Nichols, in which he relinquished his marital rights and was released from the obligation of his wife's support. The agreement likewise freed Josiah from providing financial support for their daughter, Derushua, and stipulated that he would not interfere "with any legacy, devise, or distribution share" of Nichols's estate. Finding himself by December 1840 "to require the assistance of a wife of sane mind," Josiah petitioned the legislature for a legal divorce. The legislature consented but crucially required Moore to continue to support Levisa as if she were still his wife.[11]

Here, as in the Browns' divorce, the conditions the legislature placed on the divorce gave a nod to coverture and the social responsibility of men to provide for the economic security of women. Joseph Brown was required to give Margaret one-third of his property to establish her economic security after divorce; thus the state affirmed his responsibility to provide and made sure (as far as they were able) that Margaret would not become a burden on the state. Similarly, Josiah was required to continue to support Levisa, even though their marriage had ended. This had practical elements. Levisa's parents would not live forever, and while she was insane she was unlikely to marry again; she stood at risk of becoming a financial burden on her community if not provided for by others. But as a resident of Massachusetts, Levisa did not threaten to become a drain on the resources of Wisconsin Territory—the importance of emphasizing the husband as head of household, as provider, was more abstract in this case than immediate. The actions of the legislature, by accident or design, affirmed the patriarchal structures of orderly society. The divorce occurred as a transaction between men—between legislators protecting a woman rendered economically disabled by illness, a husband who sought marital freedom but who was ordered to provide, and a father who welcomed his daughter back into his home in accordance with social practices that made a father's house one of the few legal places of refuge for unhappy or abused wives. The dissolution of the Moores' marriage did not threaten to upset the tenets of social order embedded in the law of domestic relations.[12]

In contrast, the terms of the Browns' divorce turned coverture and divorce law on their head. The Browns were divorced because of "the hostile incursions of the Sioux Indians" against them: it was a divorce prompted, and granted, in recognition of circumstances that would more ably have been resolved by the parties' relocation than by the legislature agreeing that their marriage should come to an end. In addition, as a married woman Margaret had no legal identity separate from that of her husband; she could not contract or sue in her own name, and had Joseph been charged on a criminal count, she would have been unable to testify against him. Yet the territorial legislature ordered that Joseph and Margaret draw up a separation agreement together, in effect recognizing a competent, and separate, legal identity in Margaret's person. To complicate matters further, the legislature recognized that the parties were "mutually desirous of dissolving the marriage contract," a clear admission of the collusion of the couple.

Such collusion ran against the principle by which divorce was a tool to punish the guilty and protect the innocent—there were no such identified parties in the Browns' divorce. Why, then, was the Browns' divorce successful, when so many other unhappy married couples enjoyed no such redress?[13]

It is perhaps easier to say what the divorce did not represent than what it did. The legislators' decision did not indicate a general belief that violence nullified the marriage contract: evidence suggests that violence was never considered cause for divorce by territorial legislators, even when that violence was committed against a husband or wife by his or her partner. Samuel Hubbard's suggestion that he had rightly left an abusive wife and should be allowed to divorce her fell on deaf ears. Nancy Shipley's 1841 petition for divorce was similarly denied. Shipley charged that her husband, John, "turned her and a small child out of his house when the weather was cold and severe and compelled her to remain out during the whole night." John further beat Nancy "with a hickory and threatened to kill her" while she was pregnant, "and often when she was in ill health compelled her to assist him in outdoor work." Nancy stated that she had suffered his abuse because she feared he would kill her if she complained, and it was not until she took refuge with friends and John pursued her, entering the friend's house "with a loaded gun in his hand, and made an assault upon her and had not timely assistance been rendered would, she believes, have killed her," that she sought a divorce. The violence Nancy Shipley faced was inextricably bound to the circumstances of her marriage—a full divorce would have granted her a release from the conditions that facilitated her abuse. Joseph and Margaret could claim no such direct relationship between divorce and the cessation of violence toward either of them, yet their petition was granted, whereas Nancy Shipley's was not.[14]

Where the Browns' situation materially differed from those of the other divorce petitioners of the era was in the intersection of their married life with the turbulent consequences of American expansion in the Upper Midwest. The Browns had been truthful in their description of a region riven by war—a fact of which Wisconsin's legislators could not have been ignorant. Subsistence patterns throughout the region had been threatened by a series of harsh winters and further disrupted when the wild rice crop failed in 1837; game was similarly scarce. This scarcity not only resulted in hunger but weakened an already fragile fur trade. In October 1837, Frederick Ayer noted that "game is becoming so scarce that they [the Ojibwe at Pokegoma] think the rising generation will not be able to kill enough to support life . . . The prices of the Trader's goods are very high, & game is becoming more & more scarce & so long as they depend on hunting for their necessary supplies of clothing &c. they must be poor." In May 1838 Thomas Williamson reported to his superiors in Boston that the Dakota around Traverse des Sioux were starving, ravaged by smallpox, and left with no game to hunt save muskrat. Muskrat was worthless to the fur companies, and many posts had begun to close. "Last fall the trading post west of us was abandoned," he wrote. "The two which were nearest to us on the South east have been forsaken this spring . . . [and t]he AFC have sent orders to the Trader at Lac Travers [sic] the only remaining post within 100 miles of us to abandon that." The subsistence and trade cycles of the region's Native groups were headed toward crisis, and relentless competition between the Dakota and Ojibwe for the remaining natural resources was a result. Warfare ensued as communities tried to defend and police the places where they hunted and gathered against those they perceived to be intruders into that space. It was in this context that the Dakota and Ojibwe communities with land east of the Mississippi River entered into treaty relation-ships with the United States.[15]

Traders had a particular interest in seeing the treaties come to pass. Long-standing government policies encouraged Indian communities to indebt themselves with traders as a means for the government to gain land cessions. As early as 1803, Thomas Jefferson said as much to William Henry Harrison: "To promote the disposition to exchange lands, we shall push our trading houses and be glad to see the good and influential individuals among them run in debt. Because we ob-serve that when these debts get beyond what individuals can pay, they're willing to lop them off by the cession of lands."[16]

Other parties had different motivations for supporting the treaty process. Lawrence Taliaferro, the Indian agent, believed a treaty would help shift the Dakota toward Euro-American-style agriculture, while speculators wanted access to the natural resources on Ojibwe and Dakota lands. Local Native communities also saw the benefit of ex-changing limited amounts of land for money and goods that could alleviate the subsistence problems they faced. In a treaty negotiated in 1837 the United States agreed to provide the Ojibwe with $9,500 in specie, $19,000 in goods, $2,000 in provisions, and several thousand dollars of financial support in the form of blacksmiths and farm-ers supplied with the tools of their trade. The Ojibwe were further promised the "privilege of hunting, fishing, and gathering the wild rice, upon the lands, the rivers and the lakes included in the territory ceded . . . during the pleasure of the President of the United States," a stipulation that protected them from being immediately removed. The Dakota treaty of that same year, negotiated in Washington, DC, stipulated that the U.S. government would invest $300,000 on the Dakota's behalf in order to provide an income of at least 5 percent to the community, forever. Annuities of $10,000 in goods, $5,500 in provisions, and $8,250 in agricultural supplies and support were to be paid to the Dakota for twenty years, while $90,000 was allocated for the coverage of debts. The Dakota were also promised $6,000 in goods after they had signed the treaty, to be delivered to them in St. Louis as they made the journey home.[17]

The ramifications of the treaties for the Dakota and Ojibwe were swift and uncompromising. Speculators interested in the ceded land's natural resources—most specifically lumber and water power—flooded the region before the treaties were ratified. Missionary William Boutwell observed in a letter to his superiors in Boston that "[t]he day after the Inds gave up their country some dozens of speculators rushed into the country & as I came through to this place I found one here who had taken possession of a mill seat & another there who had selected a pinery. Here they are in the neighborhood of Pokegoma, making preparations for speculation before the treaty is ratified. It is the opinion of several better capable of judging than myself that should the treaty be ratified another season will bring not less than 1000 speculators into the St. Croix." The speed of this settlement, coupled with a delay in the disbursement of annuities from the treaties, caused both the Dakota and Ojibwe to question the nature of the agreements they had signed. Edmund Ely, missionary to the Ojibwe at Fond du Lac, noted as early as January 1838 that "[w]hen we receive letters we are questioned concerning their topics, & whether any thing is said of the intentions of the Govt towards the Indians. Some affect to be displeased that any portion of their lands are sold, & wish the treaty annulled." In September that year, Jedediah Stevens noted that the Dakota bands at Lake Harriet "for several months past have manifested much dissatisfaction and restlessness, occasioned principally by a delay in carrying into effect the Treaty made with them last fall." Thomas Williamson, missionary at Lac qui Parle, offered the most succinct statement of all: "The Dakotas are at all times unsettled, but uncommonly so just now."[18]

Rather than alleviating competition for natural resources, the treaties increased tensions in the region and further violence ensued. In April 1838 three Dakota families—seventeen people in all—were killed by a small band of Ojibwe warriors from Leech Lake. At least two retaliatory attacks were organized by the Dakota that summer, and the following spring the Ojibwe struck back. In return, the Dakota, assembled en masse for the distribution of treaty payments, sent out war parties estimated by one American observer to number a total of "three or four hundred warriors." As many as 180 Ojibwe died in subsequent raids. Native suspicion of and acts of aggression toward traders, government officials, and missionaries also increased. In a letter in June 1838, Jedediah Stevens reported that the Dakota at Lake Harriet "have never before since we came here been as straitened for the means of subsistence as now." The result was, he claimed, "considerable dissatisfaction [directed] toward the *Govt, Agent,* traders and the whites generally . . . A trader some time since was fired upon and narrowly escaped death. Another, Louis Provensalle (a half-breed Sioux) was shot through the body and instantly expired." Thomas Williamson observed similar trends at Lac qui Parle, where the Dakota "became desperate killed nearly all the cattle and horses belonging to the post & one shot the trader [at Traverse des Sioux] with the intention of killing of which wound he has however recovered." That trader was Joseph R. Brown.[19]

The conditions described in the Browns' divorce petition to the Wisconsin legislature carried a stark reminder of the myriad instabilities at the territory's western fringe. This was the same instability

that the missionaries of the ABCFM recorded in their detailed reports back to Boston, that prompted Secretary of War Poinsett to
support the purchase of Pike's Island from Pelagie Faribault in 1838,
and that absorbed Fort Snelling's officers and their families through
the preterritorial period. The Dakota and Ojibwe had their own sense
of order and duty that did not answer to American law; by and large
they refused to become Christians; overwhelmingly they resisted the
forms of marriage and kinship Americans preferred. Even when they
could be convinced to enter into a treaty relationship with the U.S.
government and cede lands to American settlers, they considered the
bureaucratic workings of American government that followed such
negotiations to be unwieldy and unprincipled; all Americans were
suspect as a result, and violence flared toward missionaries and traders alike. This was the very real and lively backdrop to Joseph and
Margaret's petition—a country as yet sparsely settled by Americans
and absorbed by violent episodes Americans could not control, where
alternate meanings of place, family, law, and spirit thrived.

At the micro and macro level, the Upper Midwest was not an
American space, a reality captured by French cartographer Joseph N.
Nicollet in a map published for the U.S. government in 1843. In 1838
and 1839, Nicollet traveled extensively through the Upper Midwest
at the U.S. government's expense, determining the longitude and
latitude of significant geographic markers with a chronometer and
barometer and by reference to the stars. His expedition was, as Joel R.
Poinsett, secretary of war, articulated in his report to Congress in
1838, one means by which the government hoped to more ably plan
for future expansion. "We are still lamentably ignorant of the geog-
raphy and resources of our country," he wrote. "It is essential to its
defense, as well as to its improvement, that the boundaries, the course
of rivers, the size and form and obstacles to navigation of the lakes,

and the direction and height of the mountains, should be accurately determined and delineated." Indian agent Lawrence Taliaferro was even more direct: "We want information where to locate our Indians west of the Mississippi," he wrote in June 1837, as he urged his superiors to support Nicollet's journey. "[N]o man," he wrote, "is better calculated than Mr. N. to answer this, or any other subject of a Scientific nature desired by the government." John J. Abert of the Bureau of Topographical Engineers summarized other political motivations for supporting the map's creation. "It is not merely . . . that an opportunity is now offered of acquiring this information at a moderate compensation . . . but it also affords an opportunity of manifesting to the scientific world, that valuable and useful knowledge will always find a patron in the U. States." A map of the Upper Midwest might, in very real terms, define the United States as a whole.[20]

The completed map reflected much of the government's faith in its own ascendancy across the continent. Nicollet drew political boundaries upon the landscape, noting the borders of the Wisconsin and Iowa territories, the presence of the United States' military at Forts Snelling and Crawford, and new American communities in towns like Madison. Dominant features of the landscape were accurately recorded for westerners for the first time and, most significantly, labeled with European names—such as Plateau du Coteau des Prairies.

Yet for all the map suggested about the political, military, and social inroads Americans had made into the Upper Midwest, it also testified to the persistence of other cultures and other senses of place. The map showed the well-established trading posts of Traverse des Sioux and "Fort Renville," where Native, non-Native, and French-heritage people had formed economic and cultural alliances over the past hundred and fifty years. For each new settlement the map identified, it showed the location of older mixed-heritage communities such as Dubuque and Prairie du Chien—the very use of French spoke to a history that preceded that of the United States. Most tellingly, Nicollet was careful to note that vast swathes of land were still "M'dewakanton," "Wahpeton," "Warpekuyey," "Sissiton," and "Chipeway country."[21]

Joseph Brown and Margaret McCoy—as individuals, as a married couple, and as parties to a divorce—lived in this between-space, amid a landscape that held a thousand Native stories, that bore the oxcart trails of refugees, that ran wild with the course of rivers, upon which new settlers wished stone houses built. The county where the Browns claimed residence sat across the Mississippi River from what would, in nine years, be the territory of Minnesota. That county owed organizational and governmental allegiance to Wisconsin and to the territorial capital of Madison, but in cultural and practical terms it shared more with the country west of the Mississippi than with the settled areas of Wisconsin around Milwaukee and Green Bay. Fort Snelling was the closest U.S. institution to Joseph and Margaret, and their indigenous family and trade connections were all to the north and west. Their personal histories connected them to decades of intercultural interaction in the region, to the many couples of mixed cultural backgrounds who had, before them, enjoyed companionship, a sexual relationship, the birth of a child, and a livelihood connected to the fur trade without deep reverence for the application of Euro-American law. Their divorce oriented them toward a new social order, one that appealed to the organizing principles of American legislative decrees, but their petition was granted in large part because law could not yet order the Upper Midwest as a place.[22]

Laws had limited influence. Upheld, they could have compelled Joseph Brown to remain married to his wife, but by doing so legislators risked enforcing a connection between two people that could, amid the uncertain circumstances of Native unrest in the region, get Joseph or Margaret killed. Laws should have prevented Margaret from drawing up a contract to secure her divorce, but the result could have been a settlement in Joseph's favor, leaving Margaret destitute and thus a burden on the fledgling state. Laws could be used to declare the Upper Midwest "Wisconsin Territory," but they had no power to force the Dakota or Ojibwe people on its western fringes to recognize such a place. Laws could indeed help create a new world, extending to settlers the right to operate ferries, establish businesses, and found new towns, but they could not legislate away patterns of living that had existed in the region for centuries, nor govern the manner in which conflict between those two worlds would take place. The legal system that was supposed to establish order in the Upper Midwest was, in 1840, patently unable to do so. In a perfect paradox, the pursuit of social order required that the law be temporarily ignored.[23]

Pelagie Faribault's descendents in 1904.

Conclusion

O N OCTOBER 20, 1849, just six months after the creation
of Minnesota Territory by an act of Congress, the territorial
legislature founded the State Historical Society of Minnesota. The
"object of said Society," read the enabling legislation, "shall be the collection and preservation of a Library, Mineralogical and Geological
specimens, Indian curiosities and other matters and things connected
with, and calculated to illustrate and perpetuate the history and settlement of said Territory." In a speech given before the society's members
on January 13, 1851, Alexander Ramsey, governor of the territory and
president of the society, noted, "It may seem a strange thing, even to
some among our own citizens, and still strange to people, elsewhere,
that a *Historical Society* should have been formed in this Territory, less
than a year after its organization, when its history was apparently but
a few months old . . . A *Historical Society*," he exclaimed,

> in a land of yesterday! Such an announcement would indeed naturally
> excite at the first glance, incredulity and wonder in the general mind.

Well might it be exclaimed, "the country which has *no past*, can have no history"; with force could it be asked, "*where* are your *records?*" and if we even had them, it would not be surprising if it were still demanded, "what those records could possibly record?—what negotiations?—what legislation?—what progress in art or intellect could they possibly exhibit?""Canst thou gather figs from thorns, or grapes from thistles?"[1]

Ramsey and the other men who founded, attended the meetings of, and contributed to the collections of the state historical society believed that the region had a history worth preserving—more, they believed it had a history worth crafting with their own reminiscences. It was, as testified to by the memoirs, ethnographic essays, speeches, and journal entries they collected, a history in which white men were the locus of historical action, meaning, and significance. Thus, in Ramsey's estimation, Fathers Menard and Hennepin, seventeenth-century visitors to the region, marked the beginning of the territory's history, followed by La Hontan, Le Sueur, and Carver. "Still later," wrote Ramsey, "and within the present century, CASS and SCHOOL-CRAFT, NICOLLET and FREMONT, LONG and KEATING, have visited and explored our land; and PIKE, too, the heroic ZEBULON PIKE . . . These are our records," he wrote, "these in part, our historiographers. Their works form stepping stones, across at least that portion of the river of time, which in this region, for about two hundred years, had rolled its tide occasionally within view of the white race."[2]

There were Native people in the history to which the early society members were willing to accede, but their stories were valuable only as a precursor to the disappearance of Native communities from the region. Ramsey urged the society's members to "secure the fleeting memorials of the *red* nations who have played their parts on this division of the world's great stage" as a prerequisite to telling the tales of "the white pioneers of the North-West, who for many a year have toiled and struggled with the difficulties of the wilderness,—men of intelligence and energy and fortitude." Henry Sibley, in an 1850 address to Congress reprinted in the annals of the society, admitted that Native people still had their "forest home" in the state, "hitherto secure from the intrusion of the pale faces," but he warned that "the large and warlike tribes of Sioux and Chippewas, who now own full nine-tenths of the soil of Minnesota, must soon be subjected to the operation of the same causes that have swept their Eastern brethren from the earth." In an address written for the society in December that same year, Stephen Riggs suggested that the region's Native communities were utterly endangered. "Civilization, as it passed onward, must encircle them with its blessing, or sweep them from the face of the earth. They must be civilized and christianized or perish." Thus, when Edward Neill offered his essay "Dakota Land and Dakota Life" to the society it was to preserve a colorful chapter in the region's history that he believed to be closed. "Where but a short time since, it was no uncommon sight to see from our windows only the cone-shaped teepee, and the savage hunter with his family and dogs, we now also behold, by night, the candle in the rude log cabin sending its rays across the stream, and listen, by day, to the cheerful voice of the wood-cutter's ax, or the lullaby of the pale-faced mother, and see those engaged in household duties whose early life was passed in the schools of the East."[3]

Few women warranted mention in the narrative that the region's men were crafting. In the first volume of the society's published collections, ten women were listed as teachers in an overview of schooling in the territory, but no further details of their lives were recorded.

The reminiscences of Charlotte Van Cleve and the experiences of Abigail Snelling were used to illuminate the conditions under which the officers of the Fifth Infantry lived and worked in the first years in the region, but the enslaved women who worked for them went unacknowledged. Missionaries, clergy, diplomats, and explorers all had their place in the society's collections, but there was no such place for their daughters or wives. Perhaps most notably, many of the society's members were fur traders whose livelihoods had depended on their female Dakota and Ojibwe kin, yet in the reminiscences that lauded such men, their wives were entirely missing. Henry H. Sibley dwelled for some time on the subject of the fur traders who were "most intimately identified with the early history of Minnesota" in an 1856 address before the society. "Perhaps no body of men have ever been so misunderstood and misrepresented," he suggested. "There is an unwritten chapter yet to be contributed to the records of the Northwest, which will place the Indian trader in a proper light before the country." That light, as Sibley understood it, was meant to shine on the fortitude and entrepreneurship of male traders, but not on their families or other intimate relationships.[4]

The early members of the Minnesota Historical Society were engaged in nothing less than building a history of the region that valorized their own contributions and minimized the contentious history of white, Native, and mixed-heritage interaction before the territory came to be. The first edition of *Collections of the Minnesota Historical Society*, an abridged reprint of the society's earliest annals, was issued in 1872; by 1873, Henry Sibley was claiming for the state a history it had never enjoyed. "[T]he settlement of Minnesota has been singularly free from the disorders and deeds of violence, which have almost invariably accompanied the same process in other western territories and States," he wrote. While "reckless" migrants had snubbed Minnesota in favor of the gold fields of California, he asserted, "men who had it in view to gain a subsistence by honest labor, sought the fertile prairies of Minnesota with their families." Furthermore, he continued, "the State has been vastly benefited by remaining free from the persons who are popularly said to 'live by their wits'" and as a result Minnesota avoided "those scenes of sanguinary violence, which have disgraced the earlier history of so many of the border States." This from a man who had commanded troops in the U.S.–Dakota War of 1862.[5]

To turn our attention toward marriage—toward intimate relationships weighted with public and political significance—is to reclaim a more complex history of the region than early territorial and state leaders wanted to preserve. Examining the relationships into which women entered, however those relationships were solemnized, radically shifts our perspective on the early nineteenth-century Upper Midwest. When we put Pelagie Faribault at the center of our story we uncover the dynamics of Dakota kinship, fur trade marriage, and friendship that underwrote the machinations of U.S. diplomacy. With Mary Riggs as our entry point into the work undertaken by missionaries at Lac qui Parle we gain a new understanding of how vital marriage and gender roles were to both U.S.–sponsored imperialism and Dakota resistance to it. With Abigail Snelling, Ann Adams, and Harriet Robinson as our guides to the households of Fort Snelling we gain a fresh perspective on the importance of domestic labor to U.S. attempts to "civilize" the West and on the inconsistencies of marriage and slavery as twin institutions at the fort. With Margaret McCoy as our focal point we glimpse the complicated reality of marriage and sexual relationships in a mixed upper midwestern community and the limits of Euro-American law to order the places into which the United States wished to expand.

We also gain a fresh perspective on the men with whom these women were associated—men Henry Sibley hoped to illuminate in the "proper light" of national attention. Jean Baptiste Faribault was, in Sibley's estimation, "emphatically one of the pioneers of Minnesota," who weathered several misfortunes in his early trading life before building a successful trading venture. We know him also as a father and husband; as a man who saw no reason to solemnize his marriage to Pelagie under Euro-American law; who relied upon his wife as hostess, domestic worker, mother, and Dakota kin to underwrite his years in the trade; and who upheld her Dakota claim to Pike's Island long after her death. Joseph Brown, wrote Sibley in 1856, was notable for having "brought down the first raft of pine lumber that ever descended the St. Croix river" and for working steadfastly in the trade for more than thirty years. We can flesh out this picture and add Brown's philandering, his adultery, his eye for economic advantage in each of his marriages, his deference to the legal culture of Madison, Wisconsin, and the cost he incurred to separate from his second wife. Sibley counted Philander Prescott as an important figure in the region's fur trade—as might we, for the two marriages into which he entered with the same woman, for what his actions tell us about an encroaching American state, and for the interpersonal consequences of his insistence on a Euro-American wedding ceremony that his wife felt "a little unpleasantly" about.

We can learn a great deal about the men who consciously fashioned their version of Minnesota's history by considering the stories of their intimate relationships. Stephen Riggs claimed prominence before the members of the historical society for his expertise in the Dakota language. That expertise was not merely the result of his own study but the product of his marriage—Mary's labor had freed Stephen from having to think of his meals, his laundry, the upkeep of his home, or the care of his children while he worked. Mary's efforts to teach knitting, sewing, and weaving to local Dakota women resulted in what Riggs and his colleague Thomas Williamson both claimed as a major step forward in civilizing the Dakota people—the production of cloth on the mission station's loom. Williamson himself claimed expertise in the history of the region's early Native communities, publishing "Who Were the First Men?" in 1856. His information was based on hours of study and conversation with the Dakota people of Lac qui Parle, Kaposia, and Yellow Medicine, all made possible by the labor of Margaret, his wife. Sibley himself claimed an identity as an upstanding American gentleman—the squire of Mendota, as he came to be known before the territory was formed—who married Sarah Steele, a white woman, in a Euro-American ceremony in 1843. Yet this marriage was predated by his relationship with Red Blanket Woman, which resulted in the birth of a daughter Sibley supported for the rest of his life.[6]

A focus on marriage also asks us to consider the lasting importance and tenacity of Native marital practices through this period. Where the historical society's founders saw a story of the inevitable decline and disappearance of Native people, we can see the resilience of Native kinship practices and gender-role behavior even as Euro-Americans targeted them. We also realize the highly political nature of Euro-American marriage—of the differing rights and responsibilities awarded to men and women by the practice of coverture, and how such practices were intimately connected to the workings of the American state. The clash over marital practices at places like Lac qui Parle becomes more than a question of differing cultural values and is revealed instead to be about the lifeblood of two different political systems. Treaties and the letters of missionaries about the hardships faced by Native people give us one narrative about Native life in the Upper Midwest; the persistence of Native marriage practices and kinship systems tells us another.

Marriage, however solemnized and of whatever duration, existed at the heart of each community that met in the Upper Midwest. Marriages were entered into for various reasons—affection, duty, economic advantage, religion—and, in transforming individuals into husbands and wives, awarded each with clear responsibilities toward their new household. Women of all cultural groups labored in and around the home, but only Native women owned those spaces. Men took on political, diplomatic, and economic responsibility for their households in whatever fashion had cultural sanction within their own community—thus Dakota men would not hoe corn, and Euro-American missionaries had only one wife. The life that spouses shared might run smooth—lauded in poetry, honored with gifts—but might also run rough, through adultery, fraud, misunderstanding, or the loss of a child. Some marriages ended—a tipi moved, a divorce sought, a spouse who died—but others took their place. Marriage sorted kin from outsiders, enemies from friends, converts from resisters, women from men; it created order as a personal relationship, a building block of community, and a tangible link to nation and state. Marriage ran through the social, economic, and political culture of the Upper Midwest no less readily than waterways dissected, connected, and nourished the landscape.

※⟨✕ ⅀⟩⁊

In 1995, Virginia Driving Hawk Sneve published *Completing the Circle*, the story of her family told through oral history, photographs, poetry, and prose. There she preserved her grandmother Flora Driving Hawk's telling of the story of White Buffalo Calf Woman, a story rooted in the sacred landscape of the Dakota. "They say [Flora's stories always began] that somewhere over by the Pipestone Quarries [in present-day Minnesota], the people gathered to pray to Wakantanka," Flora recalled. In response, a woman from the Buffalo People—"a beautiful girl all dressed in white"—visited the community to dispense advice for how they should live.

> She talked to the women. "My sisters," she called them, "you have hard things to do in your life. You have pain when you have babies, and it's hard to raise children. But you are important, because without you there would be no people. So you will have babies for your husband. You will feed your man and children; you will make their clothes; you will make the tepees. You will be good wives."[7]

To some degree or another these were the tenets by which all women of the Upper Midwest lived in the early nineteenth century—they entered into marriage, were transformed from women into wives, worked hard within the home, had children, and raised them to perpetuate the traditions of their parents. Without them, to paraphrase Flora Driving Hawk, there would be no people—not merely in terms of the children they might bear, but in terms of the rights, responsibilities, and obligations they created in themselves and their partners when they took on the identity of wife. "You are important," said White Buffalo Calf Woman to the married Dakota women she visited that day. You are important, we echo to the Native, mixed-heritage, and non-Native women of the Upper Midwest; to their daughters and granddaughters; to their descendants to this day.

Acknowledgments

I could not have imagined when I first encountered Margaret McCoy in the microfilm reading room of the University of Wisconsin–Milwaukee that many years later her story would give shape to the pages of this book. I had little idea of the adventure I was beginning; little idea, too, of how many people would support me along the way. This book is the product of patience, kindness, curiosity, and friendship, and it gives me enormous pleasure to thank those who have helped and guided me as I worked.

The Alice E. Smith Fellowship from the State Historical Society of Wisconsin funded my earliest explorations of Joseph and Margaret Brown's divorce, thereby launching this entire project. A grant from the Newberry Library/CIC-American Indian Studies Consortium allowed me to attend a Newberry workshop on Borderlands, where my research and writing greatly benefited from discussing my work with my peers under the thoughtful guidance of Ned Blackhawk. The University of Iowa's Department of History supported my research by awarding me the Charles Strong Research Fellowship, and a Seashore

Fellowship from the University of Iowa supported a year spent writing my dissertation. More recently, generous support from the Edgar S. and Ruth W. Burkhardt Fund for History, and funding from the College Faculty Career Enhancement Grant, awarded to Knox College by the Andrew W. Mellon Foundation, supported me in further research in Wisconsin and Minnesota and in time spent writing this book.

I owe a great intellectual debt to my mentors who guided me through the early process of research and writing. Linda K. Kerber taught me the finer details of feminist theory, as well as the practical business of analyzing documentary silences to find women's stories. I owe her particular gratitude for both showing and teaching me to write as clearly as I can. She has been an unwavering ally in all my ventures over the past fifteen years, and I am deeply grateful for that support. Malcolm Rohrbough taught me to sort through competing theories of what was West to craft my own sense of Minnesota as a distinct, important place. He was always a voice of calm and reason and taught me to take real joy in my work. Jacki Rand made me think seriously about what I wanted my first book to be, taught me to listen for the Native voice in documents crafted to fulfill some other end, and helped me think through some of the thorniest questions my research posed. Her good humor and energy were infectious. Lastly, Brenda Child, who first introduced me to American Indian history some twenty years ago, gave me the tools to begin this long process and has become a friend and colleague whose support I value deeply.

I often say that my education began again when I started my professional life at Knox College. To the colleagues from so many other departments who have helped me think expansively about music, art, biology, literature, and more—Mark Holmes, Sarah Day O'Connell, and Natania Rosenfeld chief among them—I am blessed to be learning from you every day. My colleagues in the Department of History have been wonderfully supportive of my research since day one and have cheered this book to its completion—Danielle Fatkin, Penny Gold, Konrad Hamilton, Mike Schneider, Emre Sencer, and George Steckley, I thank you for creating and sustaining the community we share. Numerous other colleagues have supported me through the writing of this book: thanks to Katie Adelsberger, Emily Anderson, Lawrence Breitborde, Diana Cermak, Gail Ferguson, Gina Franco, Lori Haslem, Claire Falck, and Malagi Roy-Fequiere.

This book would not exist were it not for the help and support I have received from numerous archivists, librarians, and research assistants. I cannot say enough good things about the experience of researching at the Minnesota History Center—everyone, from the volunteer greeter at the door to the friendly team of research librarians who fielded my stranger questions with great aplomb, made me feel welcome. Debbie Miller was particularly helpful, and I am indebted to her astonishing memory, problem-solving skills, and constant good cheer. At Knox, the library staff have supported me in every way imaginable, and I particularly thank Laurie Sauer for helping me find obscure sources at a moment's notice and patiently creating the index for this book. I must also thank the Edwin Winslow and Mary Elizabeth Hand Bright Book Fund for making it possible to buy library holdings in pre-1848 American history. I am grateful for the diligence, patience, and creativity of all my research assistants: Devin Harvie, Bethany Otremba, and Kate Robbins. I particularly thank Kate, who undertook the exhaustive process of ordering my hundreds of photocopies into carefully indexed files for Fort Snelling, each mission station, and the Indian Agency at St. Peter's. She did this and other projects with amazing good humor, and writing this book would have been quite impossible without her.

Ann Regan at the Minnesota Historical Society Press has been a wonderful editor—insightful, thoughtful, and encouraging in turn. Shannon Pennefeather skillfully shepherded this book through production, and I am grateful for the patience and good humor she showed in answering all my questions. I also thank Pamela McClanahan for welcoming me into the press's cohort of authors and Anne Kaplan for her cheerful demeanor and deft editing of my work for *Minnesota History*. I also thank the reviewers who helped make this a better book.

I am blessed to have been supported in this venture by a legion of good friends. Jenn Dowell cheered me every step of the way and generously proofread every inch of this manuscript more than once. Laura Jones's wisdom and cheerfulness were never more than a phone call away. Ann Marie McNamara gave me shelter in every way possible. Laura Sayles welcomed me into her home in Minneapolis and more than once gave up her Saturdays to help me research. Megan Scott made me a lot of dinners and shared the everyday comfort of her porch and fine conversation in all seasons. Yvonne Seale generously offered her historical ear as I thought through the more difficult problems in my research. I owe a debt of gratitude to many others, including Rachel Barenblat, Gina Berardesco, KellyAnn Bessa, Lacy Boggs, Cynsa Bonorris, Laura Bush, Alison Feeney, Elise Fillpot, Jennifer Harbour, Melinda Jones-Rhoades, Tom LaTour, Katherine Lynn, Beth McNamara, Michelle Owens, Carrie Simmons, Amber Smigiel, Anne Taylor, Roger Taylor, Brian Tibbets, Sylvia Tremblay, Tisha Turk, Karen Whittaker, and Lisa Witte.

Finally, to my family, thank you for everything.

Notes

Notes to Introduction

1. *American*, here, describes all those people living in North America, whether U.S. citizens or immigrants, who had allied themselves with U.S. cultural, economic, and political beliefs.

2. Quote: Letter from Abigail Adams to John Adams, 31 March–5 April 1776, *Adams Family Papers*. As Abigail summed up in a letter to Mercy Otis Warren, with John away, "I find it necessary not only to pay attention to my own in door domestick affairs, but to every thing without, about our little farm &c.": Abigail Adams to Mercy Otis Warren, April 13, 1776, in *Founding Families*. For a sampling of Abigail's responsibilities, see Letters from Abigail Adams to John Adams, 16 July and 8–10 September 1775; 2–10 March, 31 March–5 April, and 7–11 April 1776, *Adams Family Papers*.

3. Blackstone, *Blackstone's Commentaries*, 2:441. See also Kerber, *No Constitutional Right to be Ladies*, 13–15; Hartog, *Husband and Wife in America*, 106–7. While small, the Massachusetts figures reflect an upward trend in the number of divorce petitions received by the governor and council of Massachusetts—a trend that would continue through the Revolutionary War. Eighty-six petitions were received between 1775 and 1786 and sixty-one granted. Cott, "Divorce and the Changing Status of Women in

Eighteenth-Century Massachusetts," 592. Divorce was the only legal remedy by which individuals might end a marriage, but extralegal agreements and separations were common remedies for situations the law could not, or would not, address: see Hartog, *Husband and Wife in America*, 1–92.

4. Letter from John Adams to Abigail Adams, 14 April 1776, *Adams Family Papers*; Gelles, *Abigail Adams*.

5. Letters from Abigail Adams to John Adams, 31 March–5 April, 7–11 April, 14 April, and 7–9 May 1776; Letter from John Adams to Abigail Adams, 28 April 1776, *Adams Family Papers*.

6. Hobbes, *Leviathan*; Locke, *Two Treatises on Government*; Rousseau, *The Social Contract and Discourses*.

7. Pateman, *The Sexual Contract*; Rousseau, "A Discourse on the Origin of Inequality" (1754), in *The Social Contract and Discourses*, 183. Indeed, Rousseau ensnared himself in this contradiction, holding that it was not until after the family was created that men and women's habits of existence began to differ. He did not explain how a woman, acting in accord with the tenets of self-preservation, would therefore get pregnant in the first place (210–11). Hobbes, *Leviathan*, 84.

8. Paine, *Common Sense*, 12, 33, 44.

9. *Journals of the Continental Congress, 1774–1789*, 4:342. Congress approved the resolution but referred it to committee for a preamble to be written. The preamble was approved on May 15: *Journals*, 4:357–58. See Thorpe, ed., *The Federal and State Constitutions*, for the constitutions of Connecticut, Delaware (Vol. 1), Georgia (Vol. 2), Maryland, Massachusetts (Vol. 3), New Hampshire, (Vol. 4), New Jersey, New York, North Carolina, Pennsylvania (Vol. 5), Rhode Island, South Carolina (Vol. 6), and Virginia (Vol. 7). See also Nash, *Unknown American Revolution*, 264–305.

10. John Adams, for example, believed that female suffrage (as well as that of men who lacked property or were below the age of twenty-one) would "confound and destroy all Distinctions, and prostrate all Ranks, to one common Levell . . . Depend upon it, sir, it is dangerous to open So fruitfull a Source of Controversy and Altercation, as would be opened by attempting to alter the Qualifications of Voters." Letter from John Adams to James Sullivan, May 26, 1776, *Papers of John Adams*, 4:212.

Zagarri, *Revolutionary Backlash*, 3037; Nash, *Unknown American Revolution*, 288–90. John McCurdy argues that the concept of the male citizen underwent significant changes in the years leading up to the Revolution. Dependency and independence became meaningful oppositions at work in men's lives (especially for bachelors), supplementing the old opposition between a man who was head of household and a man who was not. For women, however, little changed—they spent most of their lives as the legal dependents of their fathers and husbands and stepped outside that identity only as single, adult women or widows. McCurdy, *Citizen Bachelors*. See also Pascoe, *What Comes Naturally*, 22–27; Kann, *A Republic of Men*; Kerber, *Women of the Republic*.

11. Holton, *Unruly Americans and the Origins of the Constitution*; Berkin, *A Brilliant Solution*; Nash, *Unknown American Revolution*, 366–422; Jan Wilson, "Representation of Women in the Constitution," in Schwartzenback and Smith, eds., *Women and the United States Constitution*, 23–33.

12. Reginald Horsman, "The Indian Policy of an 'Empire for Liberty,'" 37–61, and Theda Purdue, "Native Women in the Early Republic: Old World Perceptions, New World Realities," 85–87, both in Hoxie, Hoffman, and Albert, eds., *Native Americans and the Early Republic*; Prucha, *American Indian Policy in the Formative Years*, 41–65.

13. Henry Knox to George Washington, July 7, 1789, *American State Papers: Indian Affairs*, 1:53.

14. Kappler, *Indian Affairs*, 2:31, 36, 42, 67–68; An Act to Regulate Trade and Intercourse with the Indian Tribes, March 1, 1793, ch. XIX, 1 *Stat.* 331; An Act Making Provision for the Purposes of Trade with the Indians, 1795, ch. LI, 1 *Stat.* 442; An Act to Regulate Trade and Intercourse with the Indian Tribes and to Preserve Peace on the Frontiers, May 19, 1796, ch. XXX, 1 *Stat.* 472. Later acts regulating trade with American Indian communities repeated, in some form or another, the provisions of the 1793 act. See An Act to Regulate Trade and Intercourse with the Indian Tribes and to Preserve Peace on the Frontiers, March 3, 1799, ch. XLVI, 1 *Stat.* 746–47; and An Act to Regulate Trade and Intercourse with the Indian Tribes and to Preserve Peace on the Frontiers, March 30, 1802, ch. XIII, 2 *Stat.* 143.

Kappler, ed., *Indian Affairs*, 2:28, 70–71, 83, 86, 93, 95.

15. Cott, *Public Vows*, 25; Purdue, "Native Women in the Early Republic," 85–122.

16. Kappler, *Indian Affairs*, 2:143. Slight differences in dower rights existed between the colonies and, later, the states; courts also had a hand in defining what a widow would actually receive. For a more detailed analysis, see Salmon, *Women and the Law of Property in Early America*, 4–9; Kerber, *Women of the Republic*, 46–48.

17. "October 14th," Diary of Jedediah Stevens, September 9, 1829, to April 2, 1830, American Board of Commissioners for Foreign Missions Papers (hereafter ABCFM), Minnesota Historical Society (hereafter MHS).

18. For considering the importance of place to human understandings of history, I am indebted to Keith Basso's *Wisdom Sits in Places: Landscape and Language Among the Western Apache*, especially 3–35.

19. Bray and Bray, *Joseph N. Nicollet*, 13, 48, 57, 64, 66, 77, 78, 86, 88–90, 102, 103, 113; Pond, *The Dakota or Sioux in Minnesota*, 17, 26–27, 30, 37–39, 43–53, 56, 58–59; Warren, *History of the Ojibway People*, 103, 175–76, 186, 263–67; "Thus Eve [July 12]," Boutwell Journal, June 12 to August 15, 1832, W. T. Boutwell to David Greene, January 18, 1837, Journal of G. T. Sprout [1837], and T. S. Williamson to H. Hill, May 30, 1836, all ABCFM, MHS. For general comments on Native agricultural practices in the western Great Lakes, see Sleeper-Smith, *Indian Women and French Men*, 73–97.

20. Warren, *History of the Ojibway People*, 76–81. The contention of historians that the Ojibwe nation did not become distinct from other Native communities (particularly the Ottawa and Potawatomi) until the late sixteenth and early seventeenth centuries is congruent with the Ojibwe's own perspective: the Wisconsin Cartographer's Guild, *Wisconsin's Past and Present*, 10; White, *The Middle Ground*, 19; Warren, *History of the Ojibway People*, 81. While the reason for early migration is unclear, later shifts owed much to the expansion of the Iroquois throughout the Ohio valley and the consequent displacement of peoples throughout the Midwest: see Warren, *History of the Ojibway People*, 82; White, *The Middle Ground*, 1–49. Warren's mother was "three-fourths" Ojibwe, and he was raised at La Pointe, the community where his father both worked as a fur trader and

would later become Indian subagent. Warren was fluent in the Ojibwe language and had kinship ties with families across the Upper Midwest, allowing him access to and understanding of the histories he recorded. His work to record the beliefs and culture of the Ojibwe of the Upper Midwest was nevertheless motivated by the belief that the "red race" was "fast disappearing before the onward resistless tread of the Anglo-Saxon": see J. Fletcher Williams, "Memoir of William W. Warren," 9–20, and Warren's own "Preface," 23–27, both in *History of the Ojibway People*.

Dewdney, *The Sacred Scrolls of the Southern Ojibway*, 60–61; Schenck, "The Voice of the Crane Echoes Far," 19–20.

21. "Kitchi-Manitou was the creator, the Great Mystery . . . Mystery is but one of the connotations of the word *manitou*. The word has other meanings as well: spiritual, mystical, supernatural, godlike or spiritlike, quiddity, essence": Johnston, *The Manitous*, xxi. Johnston, *Ojibway Heritage*. 7–79; Hilger, *Chippewa Child Life*, 60–61; S. Hall to David Greene, October 24, 1838, ABCFM, MHS.

22. Schenck, "*The Voice of the Crane Echoes Far*," 60, 71–83; also see 55–83, and Warren, *History of the Ojibway People*, 87–88; Johnston, *Ojibway Heritage*, 61–66.

23. Waziyatawin, *What Does Justice Look Like*, 23–25. I use the most recent form of Waziyatawin's name; previously she wrote as Waziyatawin Angela Wilson. See Wilson, *Remember This!* 96. Wingerd, *North Country*, 1–13; Anderson, *Kinsmen of Another Kind*, 19–28; Bray and Bray, *Joseph N. Nicollet*, 45, 61, 69, 89, 90, 94. Also see Durand, *Where the Waters Gather and the Rivers Meet*. Chippewa is another name for the Ojibwe; Sioux another name for the Dakota.

24. Oneroad and Skinner, *Being Dakota*, 121–97; Waziyatawin, *What Does Justice Look Like*, 18–20; Wilson, *Remember This!* 174.

25. Deloria, *The Dakota Way of Life*, 8–22. "As a member of the [Dakota] tribe you have, of course, your natural father and mother and siblings; that is, all their other children, your brothers and sisters . . . But now, in addition, there are any number of men and women whom you also call father and mother, your secondary or auxiliary parents. Those 'fathers' are all the men

whom your own father calls brother or cousin. They are not your uncles; only your mother's brothers and cousins are your uncles. And those 'mothers' are the women whom your mother calls sister or cousin. They are not your aunts; only your father's sisters and cousins are your aunts. Now you can see where you get so many other brothers and sisters besides your own, and where you get so many cousins": Deloria, *Speaking of Indians*, 25–26; also see 115.

26. Wingerd, *North Country*, 1–74; Skinner, *The Upper Country*.

27. Parker, "Henry Leavenworth: Pioneer General," 58–61; Leavenworth and Leavenworth, *A Genealogy of the Leavenworth Family*, 151–52.

28. This is an abbreviated version of an Ojibwe story told by Basil Johnston in *Ojibway Heritage*, 109–18.

Notes to Chapter One

1. "Original grant, by Sioux Indians, of a tract of land in the vicinity of Fort Snelling," appended to *A Statement and Explanation of the Origin and Present Condition of the Claim of Pelagie Faribault* (Washington, DC: Union Office, 1856), Graff Collection, Newberry Library. Hansen, *Old Fort Snelling*, 26–28. Despite the change in the Fort's name in 1825, I use "Fort Snelling" throughout for consistency's sake. Similarly, I use "Faribault" as the consistent spelling of Jean Baptiste and Pelagie's family name. Various spellings of their name abound in archival sources, including Ferribault, Feribault, Farribault, and Feribo.

2. "Original grant, by Sioux Indians, of a tract of land in the vicinity of Fort Snelling."

3. "The United States to Jean Baptiste Faribault and Pelagie Faribault, his wife," order of payment from the U.S. Treasury Department, 3rd Auditor's Office, February 6, 1858, Pike Island Claim File, Fort Snelling, Minn., Papers 1814–1938, MHS.

4. Prucha, *Broadax and Bayonet*, 14–33; Anderson, *Kinsmen of Another Kind*, 98–102.

5. Copy of Treaty made by Lieutenant afterwards General Z. M. Pike with the Sioux Indians (1805), Pike Island Claim File. One of the

signatories of the 1805 treaty was Little Crow, who also signed the 1820 agreement with Leavenworth. Zebulon Pike to James Wilkinson, St. Pierre 23d Sept. 1805, in Jackson, ed., *Journals of Zebulon Montgomery Pike*, 237.

6. Pike to Wilkinson, Sept. 23d, in Jackson, *Journals of Zebulon Montgomery Pike*, 237–41; Hollon, *The Lost Pathfinder*, 54–72; Wingerd, *North Country*, 80–82.

7. Wingerd, *North Country*, 81.

8. Hollon, *The Lost Pathfinder*, 51–53.

9. See Deloria and DeMallie, *Documents of American Indian Diplomacy*, 1:6–11; Meron, "The Authority to Make Treaties in the Late Middle Ages," 1–20; Saliha Belmessous, "Wabanaki Versus French and English Claims in Northeastern North America, c. 1715," 107–28, and Craig Yirush, "'Chief Princes and Owners of All': Native American Appeals to the Crown in the Early-Modern British Atlantic," 129–151, both in Belmessous, ed., *Native Claims*.

Pike, "25th Septr., Wednesday," Journal of the Mississippi River Expedition, in Jackson, *Journals of Zebulon Montgomery Pike*, 38. In 1835, Secretary of War Lewis Cass requested a full search of the Department of State's archives in order to find out if the 1805 treaty had been ratified and authorized by the president—no one knew for sure. The Department of State's eventual report was blunt: "No evidence has been found that the treaty made with the Sioux Indians, in 1805, was sanctioned by the president, and officially declared to be in force." Asbury Dickins to Lewis Cass, Washington, September 1, 1835, Pike Island Claim File. Anderson, *Kinsmen of Another Kind*, 79–81, 99.

10. J. C. Calhoun, Secretary of War, to Henry Leavenworth, December 29, 1819, emphasis in original, Pike Island Claim File; Hollon, *The Lost Pathfinder*, 51–53. Historical meteorological data provided by the Climatology Working Group at the University of Minnesota: see "Annual Climatological Study, Ft. Snelling, MN, Year 1820," at http://climate.umn.edu/doc/twin_cities/Ft%20snelling/1820sum.htm (accessed June 26, 2012). Charlotte Van Cleve (born en route to the Fort Snelling site in 1819) particularly remembered being told of a violent storm in which "the roof of our cabin [at

Cantonment New Hope] blew off, and the walls seemed about to fall in. My father . . . held up the chimney to prevent a total downfall": Van Cleve, *Memories of Fort Snelling*, 18.

11. Van Kirk, *Many Tender Ties;* Brown, *Strangers in Blood;* Murphy, *A Gathering of Rivers;* White, *The Middle Ground.* See also Wingerd, *North Country*, 125–28 and Plate 22 (with accompanying note).

12. As with many names from this period, the spelling of Joseph Ainse's last name varies widely from document to document; it is often recorded as Ainsé, Ainsse, Hanse, and Hainse. Ainse was the most common spelling in the documents I examined. For details of the Ainse family's background, see Rentmeester and Rentmeester, *The Wisconsin Creoles*, 187.

Anderson, *Kinsmen of Another Kind*, 67–69, 71–72; Sibley, "Memoir of Jean Baptiste Faribault," 173; Tableau Généalogique de la Famille Faribault Branche Canadienne and Famille Faribault Huit Generations 1669–1937, Faribault Family Genealogies, MHS.

13. Rentmeester and Rentmeester, *The Wisconsin Creoles*, 244; Sibley, "Memoir of Jean Baptiste Faribault," 168–77; Anderson, *Kinsmen of Another Kind*, 67.

14. Tableau Généalogique de la Famille Faribault; Records from the Alexander Faribault Bible, Volume 36, Genealogical Collection, MHS. For information on Alexander's career in the fur trade, see Gilman, *Henry Hastings Sibley*, 69, 113; Parker, ed., *The Recollections of Philander Prescott*, 130–31; Anderson, *Kinsmen of Another Kind*, 153; Sibley, "Memoir of Jean Baptiste Faribault," 173–79.

15. For the perspective of regional American women on their domestic responsibilities, see Riggs, *A Small Bit of Bread and Butter;* Kinzie, *Wau-bun.* For analysis of domestic work among blended, "Creole" communities, see Murphy, *A Gathering of Rivers*, 59–69. For Dakota work roles, see Spector, *What This Awl Means*, 67–77; Pond, *The Dakota or Sioux in Minnesota*, 26–31, 37–39; Hyman, *Dakota Women's Work*, 17–38.

Parker, *The Recollections of Philander Prescott*, 27; H. Leavenworth to Mr. Faribault, Cantonment at River St. Pierre, January 19, 1820, and Lawrence Taliaferro to Major J. Plympton, Northwestern Agency, St. Peter's, Upper Mississippi, July 10, 1839, Pike Island Claim File.

16. Henry Leavenworth to Jean-Baptiste Faribault, Cantonment at River St. Pierre, January 19, 1820, Pike Island Claim File; Sibley, "Memoir of Jean Baptiste Faribault," 176.

17. Taliaferro, "Autobiography," 190–99; Lawrence Taliaferro to J. C. Calhoun, June 30, 1821, Pike Island Claim File.

18. See Sibley, "Memoir of Jean Baptiste Faribault," 176; Taliaferro, "Autobiography," 198–99; Anderson, *Kinsmen of Another Kind*, 67; Gilman, *Henry Hastings Sibley*, 53.

19. See Blackstone, *Blackstone's Commentaries*, 2:441. See also Kerber, *No Constitutional Right to be Ladies*, 13–15; Hartog, *Husband and Wife in America*, 106–7.

20. Pike himself met Faribault just below the mouth of the St. Peter's River in 1805, where the latter had established camp. Pike, "21st Septr., Saturday," in Jackson, *Journals of Zebulon Montgomery Pike*, 35.

Spector, *What This Awl Means*, 67–77; Pond, *The Dakota or Sioux in Minnesota*, 26–31, 37–39; Hyman, *Dakota Women's Work*, 17–38.

21. See Gilman, *Henry Hastings Sibley*, 43–61; Goodman and Goodman, *Joseph R. Brown*, 81–122; Diary of Jedediah Stevens, September 9, 1829, to April 2, 1830, ABCFM; White and White, *Fort Snelling in 1838*, 11.

22. Parsons, *John Quincy Adams*, 193–95, 210–11; Lewis, *John Quincy Adams*, 108, 113; Fehrenbacher, *Sectional Crisis and Southern Constitutionalism*, 126–27; Feller, *The Jacksonian Promise*, 162–66; Wallace, *The Long Bitter Trail*, 50–70; 21 *Cong. Deb.* 5–8, 995–1132, 1135 (1830).

23. U.S. Supreme Court, *Worcester v. Georgia*, in Purdue and Green, eds., *The Cherokee Removal*, 70–75; Wallace, *The Long Bitter Trail*, 70–72.

24. Satz, *Chippewa Treaty Rights*, 13–17; Frederick Ayer to David Greene, Pokegoma, October 4, 1837, and Thomas Williamson to David Greene, Lac qui Parle, May 3, 1838, ABCFM. Also see Frederick Ayer to the Secretary of War, Pokegoma, September 28, 1837, William Boutwell to David Greene, Fond du Lac, November 8, 1837, and Steven Riggs to David Greene, Lake Harriet, June 22, 1838, ABCFM; Anderson, *Kinsmen of Another Kind*, 146–51.

25. Three hundred thousand dollars was invested on behalf of the Dakota, with the caveat that 5 percent of that sum be distributed annually

to the communities of the Dakota signatories. Set aside for mixed-heritage individuals connected to the villages in question was $110,000, and $90,000 was earmarked to settle Dakota debts with traders. Besides money associated with the blacksmith and agricultural operations proposed in their treaty, the Ojibwe received $9,500 in cash, $19,000 in "goods," $2,000 in "provisions," and $500 in tobacco. "Treaty with the Sioux, 1837" and "Treaty with the Chippewa, 1837," Kappler, *Indian Affairs*, 2:494, 492.

26. See summaries in J. R. Poinsett, J. B. Farribault, Pelagie Farribault, S. C. Stambaugh, Alexis Bailly, Agreement to Purchase Pike's Island, 12th March 1839, and J. R. Poinsett to S. C. Stambaugh, August 13, 1840, Pike Island Claim File.

27. Lawrence Taliaferro to J. R. Poinsett, April 19, 1839, and Lawrence Taliaferro to J. C. Calhoun, June 30, 1821, Pike Island Claim File; extract of a letter from Major J. Plympton to Brigadier General R. Jones, adjutant general United State Army, March 26, 1838, Pike Island Claim File. Representative details of the sorts of supplies brought into the fort from Prairie du Chien and St. Louis can be found in Van Cleve, *Memories of Fort Snelling*, 36; Bliss, "Reminiscences of Fort Snelling," 335, 342.

28. S. 10, 25th Cong. (1838); Cott, *Public Vows*, 52–53.

29. Lawrence Taliaferro to J. R. Poinsett, April 19, 1839, J. Plympton to T. H. Crawford, July 18, 1839, Lawrence Taliaferro to J. Plympton, July 10, 1839, all Pike Island Claim File.

30. T. Hartley Crawford to J. R. Poinsett, February 29, 1839, Pike Island Claim File.

31. T. Hartley Crawford, undated letter included in Senate Report 193, 34th Cong., 1st Sess., itself included in Ex. Doc. No. 9, "Sale of Fort Snelling Reservation," *Executive Documents Printed by Order of the House of Representatives during the Third Session of the Fortieth Congress*, 7:75l; Crawford undated letter; *Senate Journal*, 29th Cong., 1st Sess., 9 June 1846, 335; *Cong. Globe*, 34th Cong., 3rd Sess. 620 (1857); *Cong. Globe*, 33rd Cong., 2nd Sess. 581, 978–979 (1855); 34th Cong., 1st Sess. 1438 (1856); 34th Cong., 3rd Sess. 347–48, 620–21, 630, 691 (1857); "The United States to Jean Baptiste Faribault and Pelagie Faribault, his wife," order of payment from the U.S.

Treasury Department, 3rd Auditor's Office, February 6, 1858, Pike Island Claim File.

32. J. Plympton to Brigadier General R. Jones, October 19, 1837, contained in Ex. Doc. No. 9, "Sale of Fort Snelling Reservation," *Executive Documents Printed by Order of the House of Representatives during the Third Session of the Fortieth Congress,* 7:16; Wingerd, *North Country,* 157–59. The prevention of steamboats landing near the fort was, argues Wingerd, a means for Plympton and his fellow officers to gain the most from their speculation in land north of the reserve.

"Order No. 65," contained in Ex. Doc. No. 9, "Sale of Fort Snelling Reservation," 7:18; E. K. Smith to Major J. Plympton, October 19, 1837, and Joseph R. Brown to Hon. Jno. H. Tweedy, December 30, 1847, contained in Ex. Doc. No. 9, "Sale of Fort Snelling Reservation," 7:16, 19; "Case of the Fort Snelling, Minnesota, Reservation," Report of the Adjutant General's Office, Washington, April 27, 1868, contained in Ex. Doc. No. 9, "Sale of Fort Snelling Reservation," 7:3; Act of August 26, 1852, ch. XCV, 1 *Stat.* 36.

33. Rep. Com. No. 482, 33rd Cong., 2nd Sess., February 6, 1855; *Senate Journal,* 33rd Cong., 2nd Sess., 2 March, 1855, 360; Act of March 3, 1855, ch. CCIV, 2 *Stat.* 686.

34. *A Statement and Explanation of the Origin and Present Condition of the Claim of Pelagie Faribault,* 5.

35. *Cong. Globe,* 33rd Cong., 2nd Sess., 978–79 (1855); *Senate Journal,* 33rd Cong., 2nd Sess., 360 (1855). In debate in 1857, Senator Bell from Tennessee seemed quite sure that Pelagie was still alive: "Faribault, his wife and children—come here, and ask to have the benefit of your agreement with them": *Cong. Globe,* 34th Cong., 3rd Sess. 620 (1857).

36. Cong. Globe, 34th Cong., 3rd Sess., 621 (1857).

Notes to Chapter Two

1. Riggs, *Mary and I,* 25, 33, 44; Riggs, *A Small Bit of Bread and Butter,* 39, 53, 62.

2. Lucretia Longley to Alfred Longley, April 1833, Mary Longley to Alfred Longley, April 22, 1833, and Mary Ann Longley to Alfred Longley,

Thanksgiving Eve, 1834, Alfred Longley and Family Papers, MHS (hereafter ALP).

3. Mary Ann Longley to Alfred Longley, March 5, 1835, ALP; Mary Ann Longley to Alfred Longley, February 2, 1836, in Riggs, *A Small Bit of Bread and Butter*, 13.

4. Mary Ann Longley to Alfred Longley, April 26, 1836, in Riggs, *A Small Bit of Bread and Butter*, 12–13.

5. Stephen Riggs to Mary Ann Longley, quoted in Mary Ann Longley to Martha Taylor Longley, May 17, 1836, in Riggs, *A Small Bit of Bread and Butter*, 13–14.

6. February 28, 1838, in Riggs, *A Small Bit of Bread and Butter*, 66.

7. See the discussion of protestant liturgies since 1564 and the wedding liturgies from *The Prayer Book of Queen Elizabeth, 1558* and *The Liturgy of John Knox Received by the Church of Scotland in 1564*, in Seale and Stevenson, eds., *Documents of the Marriage Liturgy*, 215–38.

8. An Act for the Orderly Solemnization of Marriages, Massachusetts, 1786.

9. F. Ayer to David Greene, October 11, 1834, W. T. Boutwell to David Greene, January 23, 1835, and G. T. Sproat to David Greene, January 22, 1838, ABCFM.

10. David Greene to H. R. Schoolcraft, July 10, 1833, and David Greene to S. B. Munger, February 20 and February 21, 1834, ABCFM; Samuel W. Pond to Mrs. Sarah Pond, May 31, 1835, Pond Family Papers, MHS.

11. J. D. Stevens to Henry Hill and David Greene, January 8, 1838, S. Hall to David Greene, January 29, 1834, and L. H. Wheeler to David Greene, January 23, 1843, ABCFM. It is worth noting that Stevens's sister-in-law, Cornelia Eggleston, married a missionary herself. She and Samuel Pond (brother to Gideon Pond, based at Lac qui Parle) were married on November 22, 1838. See Stephen Riggs, "Complete List of Dakota and Ojibwa Missionaries," undated, ABCFM.

12. J. D. Stevens to Henry Hill and David Greene, January 8, 1838, Florantha Sproat to Mrs. Cephas Thompson, September 20, 1838, "Documents: La Pointe Letters," *Wisconsin Magazine of History* 16.1 (September

1932): 87; Thomas S. Williamson to David Greene, July 12, 1839, and David Greene to Stephen Riggs, April 28, 1837, ABCFM.

Mary Riggs and Sarah Poage Pond learned to dry corn from the Dakota women camped near the mission: Mary Riggs to her mother, October 8, 1837, and Mary Riggs to Alfred Riggs, September 28, 1837, in Riggs, *A Small Bit of Bread and Butter*, 50, 49. For raw materials, see supply lists, Thomas S. Williamson to David Greene, October 4, 1836, and S. Hall to David Greene, December 26, 1838, and January 1, 1841, ABCFM.

13. Thomas S. Williamson to David Greene, October 1, 1836, and July 12, 1839, Thomas S. Williamson to H. Hill, May 30, 1836, Thomas S. Williamson to David Greene, July 12, 1839, ABCFM; Mary Riggs to her parents, October 8, November 2, November 31, December 15, and December 28, 1837, May 2, 1838, January 18, 1840, and March 27, 1841, and Mary Riggs to Alfred Riggs, September 28, 1837, Thomas S. Williamson to David Greene, December 30, 1839, Mary Riggs to Thomas and Joseph Longley, November 24, 1837, and Mary Riggs to her mother, October 14, 1839, in Riggs, *A Small Bit of Bread and Butter*, 50, 54, 56, 58–59, 49, 60, 70–71, 107, 112, 149; Riggs, *Mary and I*, 65.

14. Mary Riggs to her parents, May 2, 1838, in Riggs, *A Small Bit of Bread and Butter*, 69–70; see also 54.

15. Riggs, *Mary and I*, 15; Mary Riggs to her parents, May 2, 1838, in Riggs, *A Small Bit of Bread and Butter*, 51, 52, 69–70.

16. Mary Riggs to Alfred Longley, January 1, 1838, in Riggs, *A Small Bit of Bread and Butter*, 62–63.

17. Deloria, *Speaking of Indians*, 24–26; Gibbon, *The Sioux*, 99–102.

18. Deloria, *Speaking of Indians*, 27–29; Gibbon, *The Sioux*, 101.

19. Oneroad and Skinner, *Being Dakota*, 96; Deloria, *The Dakota Way of Life*, 41–61. See also Pond, *The Dakota or Sioux in Minnesota*, 134–35; Mary Riggs to Alfred Longley, January 1, 1838, in Riggs, *A Small Bit of Bread and Butter*, 62–63; Parker, *The Recollections of Philander Prescott*, 56. Although the manuscript bears the names of both Oneroad and his Anglo collaborator, Alanson Skinner, historian Laura L. Anderson's research into the lives of both men led her "to the realization that the major portion of the

monograph was the work of Oneroad. Skinner had placed his name on the manuscript following Oneroad's as a facilitating adviser and editor": Oneroad and Skinner, *Being Dakota*, xi. For information on Oneroad's great-grandfather, Mahpiyasna, see Oneroad and Skinner, *Being Dakota*, 16–17, and Bray and Bray, *Joseph N. Nicollet*, 278–79.

20. Newly married couples might set up their own home but equally might move in with either set of parents: Deloria, *The Dakota Way of Life*, 41–61; Gibbon, *The Sioux*, 101–2.

21. Thomas S. Williamson to David Greene, October 1, 1836, and May 3, 1838, S. R. Riggs to David Greene, September 10, 1838, and March 26 and September 10, 1839, J. D. Stevens to H. Hill, September 12, 1838, and S. Hall to David Greene, September 24, 1839, ABCFM; Pond, *The Dakota or Sioux in Minnesota*, 26–31, 39, 44–48, 48–51, 54–55, 60–61, 66–70; Riggs, *A Small Bit of Bread and Butter*, 122; Mary Riggs to her mother, October 8, 1837, Mary Riggs to Alfred Longley, January 1, 1838, Mary Riggs to Henrietta Longley, January 15, 1838, Mary Riggs to her parents, April 5, 1838, Mary Riggs to her mother, September 8, 1838, and October 14, 1839, Mary Riggs to Miss Hallock, April 24, 1840, in Riggs, *A Small Bit of Bread and Butter*, 50, 62, 64, 67, 80, 105, 116. For a general overview of male and female work roles, see Deloria, *The Dakota Way of Life*, 30–40; Spector, *What This Awl Means*, 66–77.

22. Mary Riggs to her mother, October 14, 1839, in Riggs, *A Small Bit of Bread and Butter*, 105.

23. Thomas S. Williamson to David Greene, August 15, 1839, ABCFM; Mary Riggs to Henrietta Longley, June 14, 1839; Mary Riggs to Thomas Longley, July 28, 1838, in Riggs, *A Small Bit of Bread and Butter*, 98, 77.

24. Mary Riggs to her mother, October 14, 1839, in Riggs, *A Small Bit of Bread and Butter*, 105. Mary's discomfort grew when her twenty-two-month-old daughter Isabella began utilizing cushions to imitate the practice of carrying burdens on her back: Mary Riggs to her parents, December 17, 1841, in Riggs, *A Small Bit of Bread and Butter*, 139.

25. Mary Riggs to Alfred Longley, January 1, 1838—in Mary's own words, "here one must be willing to divide, & subdivide, until the last morsel

is gone, if she would not be called 'mean & stingy'"—Mary Riggs to her mother, October 11, 1841, in Riggs, *A Small Bit of Bread and Butter*, 61, 137. For more on redistribution, see Deloria, *Speaking of Indians*, 68–73. For rules of the hunt that allowed for the equitable distribution of game, see Pond, *The Dakota or Sioux in Minnesota*, 49–50.

Mary Riggs to Thomas Longley, July 23, 1838, and Mary Riggs to her mother, October 11, 1841, in Riggs, *A Small Bit of Bread and Butter*, 77–78, 137. For analysis of a similar set of interactions between the Ojibwe and the ABCFM missionaries in their midst, see Kugel, *To Be the Main Leaders of Our People*, 19–53.

26. Mary Riggs to Miss Hallock, April 24, 1840, in Riggs, *A Small Bit of Bread and Butter*, 116.

27. Mary Riggs to her mother, November 5, 1839, in Riggs, *A Small Bit of Bread and Butter*, 107. Also see Mary Riggs to her parents, May 2, 1838, in Riggs, *A Small Bit of Bread and Butter*, 71; Thomas S. Williamson to David Greene, December 30, 1839, ABCFM.

28. Frederick Ayer to the Secretary of War, September 28, 1837, Frederick Ayer to David Greene, October 4, 1837, William Boutwell to David Greene, November 8, 1837, Thomas Williamson to David Greene, May 3, 1838, Steven Riggs to David Greene, June 22, 1838, ABCFM; Mary Riggs to Miss Hallock, April 24, 1840, and Mary Riggs to her parents, May 13, 1841, in Riggs, *A Small Bit of Bread and Butter*, 116, 130. In 1856, Henry Sibley noted in an address to the Minnesota Historical Society that "[t]he missionaries have zealously devoted themselves to the work allotted to them, but it is to be regretted that there has been no good result produced in the Northwest . . . commensurate with the amount of money expended and the labor bestowed upon the enterprise": Sibley, "Reminiscences," 478.

29. Riggs, *Ta′h-koo Wah-Ka′n*, 201; Mary Riggs to her parents, March 28, 1839, and February 24, 1841, Mary Riggs to Lucretia Cooley, March 18, 1839, Mary Riggs to Henrietta Longley, June 20, 1839, and April 13, 1842, Mary Riggs to her mother, August 1, 1839, in Riggs, *A Small Bit of Bread and Butter*, 92, 94, 99–101, 126–27, 143–44; Thomas S. Williamson to David Greene, July 12, 1839, postscript, and S. R. Riggs to David Greene, July 13, 1839, ABCFM.

30. Thomas S. Williamson to David Greene, August 14, 1837, ABCFM; *The New Testament of Lord and Savior Jesus Christ.*

31. Mary Riggs to Albert Longley, August 31, 1838, Mary Riggs to Miss Hallock, April 24, 1839, Mary Riggs to her parents, February 24, 1841, in Riggs, *A Small Bit of Bread and Butter,* 79–80, 116, 127. For population estimates, see Pond, *The Dakota or Sioux in Minnesota,* 5; Anderson, *Kinsmen of Another Kind,* 14–28, 162.

32. Neill, "A Sketch of Joseph Renville," 197–202; R. P. A.-G. Morice, "Rainville, Joseph," in *Dictionaire Historique des Canadiens et Métis Français de L'Ouest,* 241–42; Pond, *The Dakota or Sioux in Minnesota,* 17–19. There is some debate about the heritage of Renville's mother. While most sources stipulate that she was wholly Dakota, Nicollet believed she was Métis. The debate is in many ways purely academic: regardless of the racial or ethnic background of Renville's grandparents, his mother culturally identified herself as Dakota and lived her life as such. See Bray and Bray, *Joseph N. Nicollet,* 106–8, including 107n.

33. Bray and Bray, *Joseph N. Nicollet,* 106–8; Mary Riggs to her mother, September 18, 1837, Mary Riggs to her parents, February 22 and March 22, 1839, and Mary Riggs to Lucretia Cooley, March 18, 1839, in Riggs, *A Small Bit of Bread and Butter,* 48, 89–90, 91–92, 94; Thomas S. Williamson to H. Hill, May 30, 1836, and D. Greene to T. S. Williamson, August 11, 1836, and S. R. Riggs to David Greene, March 26, 1839, ABCFM; Riggs, *Mary and I,* 67. The missionaries explained Renville's absence to themselves and their correspondents as being effected by the promise of a Catholic priest coming to the area the following year. This interpretation, however, does not explain Renville's return to worship at the mission church in April. The proximity of his son's death seems a more compelling influence upon his behavior than the rumor that a priest might arrive twelve months or more into the future.

34. Pond, *The Dakota or Sioux in Minnesota,* 15–26; Spector, *What This Awl Means,* 41–47; Anderson, *Kinsmen of Another Kind,* 106; Kugel, *To Be the Main Leaders of Our People,* 33; Bruce M. White, "The Power of White," in Kaplan and Ziebarth, eds., *Making Minnesota Territory,* 37–38. For a

more general history of traders marrying Native women according to the customs practiced by her community, see Van Kirk, *Many Tender Ties*; Brown, *Strangers in Blood*.

35. Independent scholar Carrie Reber Zeman dates the Renvilles' second marriage to 1829: Zeman and Derounian-Stodola, eds., *A Thrilling Narrative of Indian Captivity*, 5. Neill, "A Sketch of Joseph Renville," 204.

36. Parker, *The Recollections of Philander Prescott*, 56; Mary Riggs to her grandfather, June 24, 1837, in Riggs, *A Small Bit of Bread and Butter*, 39; Goodman and Goodman, *Joseph R. Brown*, 59–61, 135, 288–92.

37. Goodman and Goodman, *Joseph R. Brown*, 66–67, 118–122; Anderson, *Kinsmen of Another Kind*, 103–49; Saler, "Negotiating the Treaty Polity."

Notes to Chapter Three

1. Frances Webster to Edmund Smith, July 26, 1845, in Baker, ed., *The Websters*, 57–58. For Ephraim's service at Fort Snelling, see White and White, *Fort Snelling in 1838*, 67.

2. Nathan Jarvis to Nathaniel Jarvis, June 1, 1833, and February 2, 1834, Nathan Jarvis Papers, MHS.

3. Josiah Snelling to Brigadier General Thomas Jessup, Quartermaster General, August 16, 1824, and Lieutenant McClure to Major General Jessup, March 1, 1835, Fort Snelling Papers, MHS; Jones, *Citadel in the Wilderness*, 49–52; Hansen, *Old Fort Snelling*, 27–30.

4. Callender, *New Light on Old Fort Snelling*; Johnson, "Fort Snelling from Its Foundation to the Present Time," 427–31; Obst, "Abigail Snelling," 102; Hamilton, "Zachary Taylor," 97–98; Bliss, "Reminiscences of Fort Snelling," 335; Eastman, *Dakotah*.

5. Van Cleve, *Memories of Fort Snelling*, 2; Bliss, "Reminiscences of Fort Snelling," 339.

6. Bliss, "Reminiscences of Fort Snelling," 335; Adams, "Early Days at Red River Settlement," 99.

7. Colonel Snelling's Account, 6th December, 16th December 1825, Vol. 7; Lieutenant Jameson's Account, November and December, 1827, Vol. 11; Captain Garland's Account, August 1827 through January 1828, Vol. 11;

Colonel Snelling's Account, December 2, 1825, Vol. 18; Lieutenant Baxley's Account, October 1825 through May 1826, Vol. 18; Captain Garland's Account, July 1828 through July 1829, Vol. 20, all in Alexis Bailly Papers, MHS; Van Cleve, *Memories of Fort Snelling,* 14–15, 26–27; Adams, "Early Days at Red River Settlement," 99; Bliss, "Reminiscences of Fort Snelling," 342.

8. Bliss, "Reminiscences of Fort Snelling," 342; Adams, "Early Days at Red River Settlement," 99; Nathan Jarvis to William Jarvis, December 31, 1834, Nathan Jarvis Papers, MHS; Van Cleve, *Memories of Fort Snelling,* 16.

9. Peter Garrioch diary, August 2, 1837, MHS, emphasis in original; David Greene to J. D. Stevens, March 19, 1834, ABCFM.

10. Allen, *Jefferson Davis,* 81–82. Allen argues that Knox's upcoming wedding was not a secret to her family—her female family members helped her make her wedding trousseau. Nevertheless, the wedding was not conducted at her family's place of residence, and no members of her family attended the ceremony. Knox openly admitted she did not have her parents' "sanction" to wed: Allen, *Jefferson Davis,* 86–88. White and White, *Fort Snelling in 1838,* 72–75.

11. Adams, "Early Days at Red River Settlement," 94–95; Featherstonhaugh, *Canoe Voyage,* 1:265, 2:6; White and White, *Fort Snelling in 1838,* 81–83; VanderVelde, *Mrs. Dred Scott,* 33, 44–46.

12. VanderVelde, *Mrs. Dred Scott,* 14, 21–25, 46–47, 74–75; White and White, *Fort Snelling in 1838,* 81–87. Lawrence Taliaferro journal, March 31, 1826, and May 29, 1829, Lawrence Taliaferro Papers, MHS; Newsom, *Pen Pictures of St. Paul, Minnesota,* 1:9; Folsom, *Fifty Years in the Northwest,* 26; Bliss, "Reminiscences of Fort Snelling," 336. See, for example, claim form, B. F. Larned, December 1, 1819; claim form, E. Purcell, December 31, 1819; claim form, Clark, October 31, 1820; claim form, Hubbs, December 31, 1820; claim form, B. Larned, December 31, 1820; claim form, Hubbs (second claim), December 31, 1820; claim form, Baxley, December 31, 1820; claim form, Snelling, December 31, 1820—all in Fort Snelling Papers, MHS.

13. *Reconstructing the Household;* Bynum, *Unruly Women;* McCurry, *Masters of Small Worlds;* Schwalm, "*A Hard Fight for We.*"

Douglass, *The Life and Times of Frederick Douglass;* Jacobs, *Incidents in the Life of a Slave Girl;* Horton and Horton, *In Hope of Liberty,* 25–26.

14. See, for example, Josiah Snelling to General Gaines, May 16, 1822, and Josiah Snelling to Brigadier General Jessup, August 16, 1824, Fort Snelling Papers, MHS; Steckle, *Topographical Sketch of Fort St. Anthony,* shows the size and location of the officers' gardens. Luecke, *Feeding the Frontier Army;* Conversation with historical reenactors, Commanding Officers' kitchens, Historic Fort Snelling, July 18, 2012. See also Commanding Officers' Quarters, Historic Fort Snelling, http://www.historicfortsnelling.org/plan-visit/what-do/commanding-officers-quarters, and Officers' Quarters, Historic Fort Snelling, http://www.historicfortsnelling.org/plan-visit/what-do/officers-quarters (accessed August 10, 2012).

15. Taliaferro journal, March 31, 1826, Taliaferro Papers, MHS; VanderVelde, *Mrs. Dred Scott,* 75, 107; Bliss, "Reminiscences of Fort Snelling," 336; Williams, "Memoir of Captain Martin Scott," 183–84.

16. Bliss, "Reminiscences of Fort Snelling," 336; Hansen, *Old Fort Snelling,* 27–28, 82; also Eastman, *Fort Snelling near Falls of St, Anthony* (graphite sketch).

17. Bliss, "Reminiscences of Fort Snelling," 341, 345; Taliaferro journal, August 21, 1829, Taliaferro Papers, MHS; Hansen, *Old Fort Snelling,* 91–92.

18. Van Cleve, *Memories of Fort Snelling,* 33; Taliaferro journal, July 3, 1835, Taliaferro Papers, MHS. There is no more accurate information on the exact date of the wedding. May 8, 1836, represents the day Emerson, with Dred, arrived at Fort Snelling, and September 14, 1837, the day that Lieutenant Thompson at the fort contracted with Emerson, rather than Taliaferro, for Harriet's services. Harriet had become a member of the extended Emerson household somewhere in between. See VanderVelde and Subramanian, "Mrs. Dred Scott," 1054–55.

19. Carroll, "'Who was Jane Lamont?'" 184–96; Carroll, "The McLeods," for the Faribaults, see Chapter One; for Prescott, see Chapter Two. White, *Guide to the Lawrence Taliaferro Papers;* VandeVelde, *Mrs. Dred Scott,* 21–42; Taliaferro, "Autobiography," 234–35.

20. See, for example, the reminiscences of Violet, an ex-slave, in Sterling, ed., *We Are Your Sisters*, 35–36.

21. See Horton, *Free People of Color*; Lebsock, *The Free Women of Petersburg*, 91–94; Schwalm, "'Overrun with Free Negroes,'" 149–51.

22. Taliaferro, "Autobiography," 134–35; VanderVelde and Subramanian, "Mrs. Dred Scott," 1033–34, 1098–99.

23. Nathan Jarvis to Mary Jarvis, February 2, 1834, Nathan Jarvis Papers, MHS.

Notes to Chapter Four

1. Goodman and Goodman, *Joseph R. Brown*, 111–12; State of Wisconsin, An Act for the Relief of Joseph R. Brown (1840); Deed of Separation of Joseph Brown & Margaret Brown (1841), Deed Book D, Crawford County (WI), Register of Deeds: Record Books, 1811–1969, Microfilm, Reel 2. The spelling of Margaret's first name varies between documents, including Margerit and Marguerite. I have used Margaret throughout for consistency's sake.

2. Petition of J. R. Brown for Divorce, Wisconsin Legislature: Petitions, Remonstrances, and Resolutions, Box 1, 1838–41, State Historical Society of Wisconsin (hereafter SHSW).

3. Goodman and Goodman, *Joseph R. Brown*, 111, 290; Gilman, *Henry Hastings Sibley*, 59; Wingerd, *North Country*, 147. Margaret's mother is named Lagrue on the record of Margaret's marriage to Joseph Bourcier in 1841: Marriage Record No 5, December 28, 1841, Parish of St. Peters, Selected records from Cathedral of St. Paul, Parish Record Books, 1840–57, MHS. For evidence of La Grue as a naming practice within French-Ojibwe circles, see Malhoit, "A Wisconsin Fur Trader's Journal," 201. For Cadotte, see Goodman and Goodman, *Joseph R. Brown*, 90; Wingerd, *North Country*, 54, 84, 154.

4. Second letter of Joseph R. Brown to Henry H. Sibley, October 4, 1836, Henry Hastings Sibley Papers, microfilm copy of original, MHS; Gilman, *Henry Hastings Sibley*, 75–76, 84–87.

5. Goodman and Goodman, *Joseph R. Brown*, 129–31, 135–36, 289, 290–92. Bouché was a witness to that deed. Baptismal records suggest that

Bouché was Adeline's father, but definitive proof comes from his listing as her parent on her death certificate from 1921: Magdeline McKye baptism record, No. 65, Parish of St. Peters, Selected records from Cathedral of St. Paul Parish Record Books, 1840–57, MHS; Adelina Sharrow certificate of death, No 22230 (1921), State of Minnesota, Division of Vital Statistics, St. Paul. [Adeline's name is variously spelled Magdeline, Adeline, Adelina, MaKye, and McCoy (before her marriage).] Marriage record No 5, Cathedral of St. Paul Parish Record Books, MHS.

6. See *Journal of the Council: Third Session of the Second Legislative Assembly of Wisconsin* (Madison, WI: William W. Wyman, 1840), 3, 4, 97, 105, 109, 111, 131, 139, 145, 154; *Journal of the House of Representatives of the Second Legislative Assembly of Wisconsin, Third Session* (Madison, WI: Josiah A. Noonan, 1840), 3, 4, 171, 187–90, 227; "The Territorial Census for 1836," 247–70; Childs, "Recollections of Wisconsin," 153–95; Jung, "Judge James Doty and Wisconsin's First Court," 32–41; Martin, "Narrative," 385–415; Pratt, "Reminiscences of Wisconsin," 127–45; Marryat, "An English Officer's Description of Wisconsin," 137–54; Dyer, "Rochester Early Settlers"; entries on Nelson, Dewey, Charles Clark Sholes, Horatio Nelson Wells, and Edward Vernon Whiton in *Dictionary of Wisconsin History*; Goodman and Goodman, *Joseph R. Brown*, 170–77.

7. "Stoner's Memories." See also Hatheway, "Surveying in Wisconsin in 1837," 390–99; Childs, "Recollections of Wisconsin," 191; Knapp, "Early Reminiscences of Madison," 374–75.

8. For general discussion of divorce in America before 1840, see Grossberg, *Governing the Hearth*; Riley, *Divorce*; Hartog, *Husband and Wife in America*, 29–33.

Michigan, An Act Concerning Divorces (1819); Michigan, An Act Concerning Divorce (1832); Wisconsin, An Act Concerning Divorce (1839). The 1819 Michigan statute allowed divorce *a mensa et thoro* if a husband had abandoned or neglected his wife. By 1832, these grounds had been replaced by "extreme cruelty" and "wilful desertion of either party for five years." By 1839, Wisconsin had reduced the term of abandonment from five to two years, reinserted "abandonment of the wife by the husband, or his refusal or neglect to provide for her," and added "habitual drunkenness" as a basis for petition.

9. Hartog, *Husband and Wife in America*; Cott, *Public Vows*, 24–55.

10. Samuel Hubbard, Affidavit and Petition, December 30, 1839, and Petition of Hariet Tyrer, December 7, 1840, Wisconsin Legislature: Petitions, Remonstrances, and Resolutions, Box 2, 1839–41; Petition of Sarah Leach for a Divorce from her Husband John Leach, January 14, 1842, and Petition of Rebecca P. Farrington, Wisconsin Legislature: Petitions, Remonstrances, and Resolutions, Box 3, 1842–43, SHSW. Also see Samuel Hubbard, Affidavit and Petition, December 30, 1839; Petition of Magdaline Gauthier for divorce, November 2, 1838 [misfiled]; Petition of Peter Howard, December 6, 1840—all in Wisconsin Legislature: Petitions, Remonstrances, and Resolutions, Box 2, 1839–41, SHSW; Petition of Sarah Leach, January 14, 1842; Petition of Adelheid Deisner, March 6, 1843; Petition of Elizabeth Harlow, March 14, 1843—all in Wisconsin Legislature: Petitions, Remonstrances, and Resolutions, Box 3, 1842–43, SHSW.

11. Petition of Peter Howard, December 6, 1840, and Petition of Josiah Moore, December 26, 1840, Wisconsin Legislature: Petitions, Remonstrances, and Resolutions, Box 2, 1839–41, SHSW; Wisconsin, An Act to divorce Peter Howard from his wife Sarah Howard, and to change the name of said Howard (1841); Wisconsin, An Act for the Relief of Josiah Moore (1841).

12. See Hartog, *Husband and Wife in America*, 97.

13. Wisconsin, An Act Concerning Divorce (1839); Wisconsin, An Act for the Relief of Joseph R. Brown, preamble (1840); Blackstone, *Blackstone's Commentaries*, 2:441. See also Kerber, *No Constitutional Right to be Ladies*, 13–15; Hartog, *Husband and Wife in America*, 79–82, 106–7.

14. Petition of Nancy Shipley for a Divorce, "Referred to the comm. on Judiciary, January 22, 1841," Wisconsin Legislature: Petitions, Remonstrances, and Resolutions, Box 2, 1839–41, SHSW.

15. See Frederick Ayer to David Greene, October 4, 1837 (it is worth noting that the missionaries always thought of Native groups as poor, judging their living patterns, as they did, in comparison to eastern Euro-American standards of dress, housing, and subsistence), Thomas Williamson to David

Greene, May 3, 1838, both ABCFM. Also see Frederick Ayer to the Secretary of War, September 28, 1837, William Boutwell to David Greene, November 8, 1837, and Steven Riggs to David Greene, June 22, 1838, ABCFM.

16. Jefferson to William Henry Harrison, February 27, 1803, as cited in Holmes, *Thomas Jefferson*, 186.

17. Wingerd, *North Country*, 128–35; Treaty with the Chippewa (1837), in Kappler, *Indian Affairs*, 2:491–93; Treaty with the Sioux (1837), in Kappler, *Indian Affairs*, 2:493–94. The treaty also promised $110,000 to mixed-heritage individuals who could claim kinship with the Dakota bands.

18. William Boutwell to David Greene, August 17, 1837, Edmund Ely to David Greene, January 5, 1838, J. D. Stevens to David Greene, September 12, 1838, and Thomas S. Williamson to David Greene, May 10, 1838; on the question of lumber speculation and land sales, also see Frederick Ayer to David Greene, October 4, 1837, all ABCFM.

19. J. D. Stevens to David Greene, July 8, 1839, ABCFM. For details of the escalating conflict between the nations, see Thomas Williamson to David Greene, May 3, 1838, J. D. Stevens to David Greene, June 28, 1838, J. D. Stevens to H. Hill, September 12, 1838, S. R. Riggs to David Greene, October 1838, S. Hall to David Greene, October 24, 1838, Jedediah Stevens to David Greene, June 28, 1838, and Thomas Williamson to David Greene, May 10, 1838, all ABCFM. For historical enmity between the Ojibwe and Dakota, see White, *The Middle Ground*, 147–48, 492, 512.

20. Report of the Secretary of War, *Congressional Globe*, 25th Congress, 3rd Sess., Appendix, 4; Lawrence Taliaferro to Carey A. Harris, Commissioner of Indian Affairs, "St. Peters," June 19, 1837, in Bray and Bray, *Joseph N. Nicollet*, 212.

21. Nicollet, *Map of the Hydrographical Basin of the Upper Mississippi River* (1843).

22. In this, Joseph and Margaret were like countless other fur trade couples before them: see Van Kirk, *Many Tender Ties*; Brown, *Strangers in Blood*; Murphy, *A Gathering of Rivers*; Sleeper Smith, *Indian Women and French Men*; Ekberg, *Stealing Indian Women*.

23. U. S. Congress, An Act Establishing the Territorial Government of Wisconsin, Statutes at Large, 5, 15, (1836). See, for example, Wisconsin, An

Act to authorize Matthias Hamm and Horace Smead to establish a ferry across the Mississippi River (1838); An Act to authorize Levi Moffett to keep a ferry across Skunk River, at Moffett's Mill (1838); An Act to authorize William H. Bruce and others to build and maintain a dam on the Manitouwoc River, and for other purposes (1840); An Act to incorporate the 'Wiscosin [*sic*] Lead Mining, Smelting and Manufacturing Company' (1840); An Act to incorporate the Fox and Wisconsin Steam Boat Company (1840); An Act to Provide for the Government of the Several Towns in this Territory, and for the Revision of County Government (1841).

Notes to Conclusion

1. An Act to Incorporate the Historical Society of Minnesota (1849), 10; Ramsey, "Our Field of Historical Research," 43–44.

2. Ramsey, "Our Field of Historical Research," 45–46.

3. Ramsey, "Our Field of Historical Research," 51; Sibley, "Description of Minnesota," 39; Riggs, "The Dakota Language," 89; Neill, "Dakota Land and Dakota Life," 254.

4. Baker, "Early School of Minnesota," 81–83; "Early Days at Fort Snelling," 420–38; Sibley, "Reminiscences," 457, 463.

5. Sibley, "Reminiscences," 273, 275.

6. Williamson, "Who Were the First Men?" 295–301.

7. Sneve, *Completing the Circle*, 3–4.

Bibliography

Archival Sources

Alexis Bailly Papers. Minnesota History Center, St. Paul.

Alfred Longley and Family Papers. Minnesota History Center, St. Paul.

American Board of Commissioners for Foreign Missions Papers. Minnesota History Center, St. Paul.

Cathedral of St. Paul. Parish Record Books, 1840–57. Minnesota History Center, St. Paul.

Crawford County (WI). Register of Deeds: Record Books, 1811–1969. Wisconsin Historical Society, Madison.

Eastman, Seth. *Fort Snelling near Falls of St. Anthony.* Graphite sketch, 1833. Negative 875. Art Collection. Minnesota History Center, St. Paul.

Fort Snelling Papers. Minnesota History Center, St. Paul.

Franklin Steele Papers. Minnesota History Center, St. Paul.

Graff Collection. Newberry Library, Chicago.

Henry Hastings Sibley Papers. Microfilm copy of original. Minnesota History Center, St. Paul.

Lawrence Taliaferro Papers. Minnesota History Center, St. Paul.

Nathan Jarvis Papers. Minnesota History Center, St. Paul.

Office of the State Registrar of Vital Records. Death certificates. State of Minnesota. St. Paul.

Peter Garrioch Diaries. Minnesota History Center, St. Paul.

Pond Family Papers. Minnesota History Center, St. Paul.

Wisconsin Legislature. Petitions, Remonstrances, and Resolutions. Wisconsin Historical Society, Madison.

Primary Sources

"An Act to Incorporate the Historical Society of Minnesota." 1849. *Collections of the Historical Society of Minnesota* 1 (1872): 10.

Acts of the Legislature of Wisconsin, Passed During the Winter Session, 1837–8, and the Special Session of June, 1838. Burlington, WI: James E. Edwards, 1838.

Adams, Ann. "Early Days at Red River Settlement, and Fort Snelling: Reminiscences of Mrs. Ann Adams." *Collections of the Minnesota Historical Society* 6 (1894): 75–116.

Adams, John. *Papers of John Adams.* Edited by Robert J. Taylor. Vol. 4. Cambridge, MA: Belknap Press, 1979.

———. *The Political Writings of John Adams: Representative Selections.* Edited by George A. Peek. 1954. Reprint, Indianapolis, IN: Hackett Publishing Company, Inc.

Adams Family Papers: An Electronic Archive. Massachusetts Historical Society. http://www.masshist.org/digitaladams/.

American State Papers: Indian Affairs. Washington, DC: Gales and Seaton, 1832.

Baker, D. A. J. "Early School of Minnesota." *Collections of the Minnesota State Historical Society* 1 (1872): 81–83.

Blackstone, William. *Blackstone's Commentaries: With Notes of Reference to the Constitution and Laws of the United States and of the Commonwealth of Virginia.* Vol. 2. Edited by St. George Tucker. 1803. Reprint, New York: Augustus M. Kelley, 1969.

Bliss, John H. "Reminiscences of Fort Snelling." *Collections of the Minnesota Historical Society* 6 (1894): 335–53.

Bracken, Charles. "Further Strictures on Ford's Black Hawk War." *Wisconsin Historical Collections* 2 (1856): 402–14.

Bray, Edmund C., and Martha Coleman Bray, eds. and trans. *Joseph N. Nicollet on the Plains and Prairies: The Expeditions of 1838–39 with Journals, Letters, and Notes on the Dakota Indians.* St. Paul: Minnesota Historical Society Press, 1993.

Childs, Ebenezer. "Recollections of Wisconsin since 1820." *Wisconsin Historical Collections* 4 (1859): 153–95.

Deloria, Ella. *The Dakota Way of Life.* Rapid City, SD: Mariah Press, 2007.

———. *Speaking of Indians.* Introduction by Vine Deloria, Jr. Lincoln: University of Nebraska Press, 1998.

Deloria, Vine, Jr., and Raymond J. DeMallie. *Documents of American Indian Diplomacy: Treaties, Agreements and Conventions, 1775–1979.* Norman: University of Oklahoma Press, 1999.

"Documents: La Pointe Letters." *The Wisconsin Magazine of History* 16.1 (September 1932): 85–95.

"Documents: La Pointe Letters." *The Wisconsin Magazine of History* 16.2 (December 1932): 199–210.

Douglass, Frederick. *The Life and Times of Frederick Douglass, An American Slave, Written by Himself.* 1845. Reprint, Boston: Bedford Books, 1993.

Dyer, Charles E. "Rochester Early Settlers." Historical address, 1871. Reprint, http://www.racinehistory.com/wrw.htm#Rochester.

"Early Days at Fort Snelling." *Collections of the Minnesota State Historical Society* 1 (1872): 420–38.

Eastman, Mary Henderson. *Dakotah: or, Life and Legends of the Sioux.* 1849. Reprint, with a preface by Rena Neumann Coen. Afton, MN: Afton Historical Society Press, 1995.

Featherstonhaugh, George W. *A Canoe Voyage Up the Minnay Sotor.* Vols. 1–2. London: Richard Bently, 1847.

Filmer, Robert. *Patriarcha and Other Political Works.* Edited by Peter Laslett. Oxford: Basil Blackwell, 1949.

Fletcher, Williams J. "Memoir of Captain Martin Scott." *Collections of the Minnesota Historical Society* 3 (1880): 180–87.

Folsom, W. H. C. *Fifty Years in the Northwest.* St. Paul, MN: Pioneer Press Company, 1888.

Founding Families: Digital Editions of the Papers of the Winthrops and the Adamses. Edited by C. James Taylor. Boston: Massachusetts Historical Society, 2007. http://www.masshist.org/ff/.

The General Laws of Massachusetts From the Adoption of the Constitution to February 1822. Boston: Wells and Lilly and Cummings and Hilliard, 1823.

Hobbes, Thomas. *Leviathan.* 1651. Edited and with an Introduction and Notes by J. C. A. Gaskin. Oxford: Oxford University Press, 1998.

Jackson, Donald, ed. *The Journals of Zebulon Montgomery Pike with Related Letters and Documents.* Norman: University of Oklahoma Press, 1966.

Jacobs, Harriet. *Incidents in the Life of a Slave Girl, Written By Herself.* Edited by Jean Fagan Yellin. 1861. Reprint, Cambridge, MA: Harvard University Press, 1987.

Johnston, Basil. *The Manitous: The Spiritual World of the Ojibway.* St. Paul: Minnesota Historical Society Press, 2001.

———. *Ojibway Heritage.* 1976. Reprint, Lincoln: University of Nebraska Press, 1990.

Journal of the Council, Third Session of the Second Legislative Assembly of Wisconsin. Madison, WI: William W. Wyman, 1840.

Journal of the House of Representatives of the Second Legislative Assembly of Wisconsin; Third Session. Madison, WI: Josiah A. Noonan, 1840.

Journals of the Continental Congress, 1774–1789. Edited by Worthington C. Ford. Washington, DC: Government Printing Office, 1904–37.

Kappler, Charles. J., ed. *Indian Affairs: Laws and Treaties.* Vol. 2: Treaties. Washington, DC: Government Printing Office, 1904.

Kinzie, Juliette Augusta. *Wau-bun: The Early Day in the North West.* 1856. Reprint, Chicago: Rand, McNally & Company, 1901.

Knapp, Joseph Gillett. "Early Reminiscences of Madison." *Report and Collections of the State Historical Society of Wisconsin* 6 (1872): 366–87.

Laws of the Territory of Michigan. Vol. I. Lansing, MI: W. S. George and Co., 1871.

Laws of the Territory of Michigan. Vol. III. Lansing, MI: W. S. George and Co., 1874.

Laws of the Territory of Wisconsin, Passed at Madison by the Legislative Assembly at its Annual Session of 1839–40. Milwaukee, WI: Harrison Reed, 1840.

Laws of the Territory of Wisconsin, Passed at Madison by the Legislative Assembly at its August Session, 1840, and its Annual Session, 1840–41. Madison, WI: W. W. Wyman, 1841.

Local Acts of the Legislature of Wisconsin, Passed at Madison during the Sessions of 1838–9. Milwaukee, WI: Daniel H. Richards, 1839.

Locke, John. *Two Treatises of Government.* 1690. Edited by Mark Goldie. London: Everyman, 1998.

Malhoit, François Victor. "A Wisconsin Fur Trader's Journal, 1804–1805." *Wisconsin Historical Collections* 19 (1910): 163–233.

Marryat, Frederick. "An English Officer's Description of Wisconsin in 1837." *Wisconsin Historical Collections* 14 (1898): 137–54.

Martin, Morgan L. "Narrative of Morgan L. Martin." *Collections of the State Historical Society of Wisconsin* 11 (1888): 385–413.

Mitchell, August, and Henry J. Abel. *Map of the Settled Part of Wisconsin Territory compiled from the Latest Authorities.* Compiled and Engraved by J. H. Young, Philadelphia. 1838. David Rumsey Historical Map Collection, San Francisco. http://www.davidrumsey.com.

Neill, E. D. "Dakota Land and Dakota Life." *Collections of the Minnesota State Historical Society* 1 (1872): 254–94.

———. "A Sketch of Joseph Renville: A 'Bois Brule' and Early Trader of Minnesota." *Collections of the Minnesota Historical Society* 1 (1872): 196–206.

The New Testament of Lord and Savior Jesus Christ, Translated out of the Original Greek, and with The Former Translations Diligently Compared and Revised, by His Majesty's Special Command. London: George Eyre & Andrew Atrahan, 1818.

Newsom, T. M. *Pen Pictures of St. Paul, Minnesota, and Biographical Sketches of Old Settlers, from the Earliest Settlement of the City, Up to and Including the Year 1857.* Vol. 1. St. Paul: The author, 1886.

Nicollet, Joseph. *Map of the Hydrographical Basin of the Mississippi River.* 1843. David Rumsey Map Collection, San Francisco. http://www.david rumsey.com.

Oneroad, Amos E., and Alanson B. Skinner. *Being Dakota: Tales and Traditions of the Sisseton and Wahpeton.* Edited by Laura L. Anderson. St. Paul: Minnesota Historical Society Press, 2003.

O'Sullivan, John L. "Annexation." *United States Magazine and Democratic Review* 17.1 (1845): 5–10.

Paine, Thomas. *Common Sense.* 1776. Reprint, New York: Penguin, 2005.

Parker, Donald Dean, ed. *The Recollections of Philander Prescott: Frontiersman of the Old Northwest, 1819–1862.* Lincoln: University of Nebraska Press, 1966.

Pike, Zebulon Montgomery. *The Expeditions of Zebulon Montgomery Pike to the Headwaters of the Mississippi River, Through Louisiana Territory, and in New Spain, During the Years 1805–06–07.* Edited by Elliot Cues. Vol 1. New York: Francis P. Harper, 1895.

Pond, Samuel W. *The Dakota or Sioux in Minnesota as They Were in 1834.* 1908. Reprint, St. Paul: Minnesota Historical Society Press, 1986.

Pratt, Alexander F. "Reminiscences of Wisconsin." *Collections of the State Historical Society of Wisconsin* 1 (1903): 127–45.

Public Statutes at Large of the United States of America. Edited by Richard Peters. Vols. 1–2. Boston: Charles C. Little and James Brown, 1845.

Ramsey, Alexander. "Our Field of Historical Research." *Collections of the Historical Society of Minnesota* 1 (1872): 43–52.

"Report of the Secretary of War." *Congressional Globe.* 25th Congress, 3rd session, Appendix, 4.

Riggs, Maida Leonard, ed. *A Small Bit of Bread and Butter: Letters from the Dakota Territory, 1832–1869.* South Deerfield, MA: Ash Grove Press, 1996.

Riggs, Stephen R. "The Dakota Language." *Collections of the Historical Society of Minnesota* 1 (1872): 89–107.

———. *Mary and I: Forty Years with the Sioux.* 1880. Reprint, Williamstown, MA: Corner House—Publishers, 1971.

———. *Ta'h-koo Wah-Ka'n, or The Gospel Among the Dakotas.* 1869. Reprint, New York: Arno Press, 1972.

Rodolf, Theodore. "Pioneering in the Wisconsin Lead Region." *Wisconsin Historical Collections* 15 (1900): 338–89.

Rousseau, Jean-Jacques. *The Social Contract and Discourses.* Translated and Edited by G. D. H. Cole, 1913. Reprint, London: J. M. Dent, 1920.

Sibley, Henry H. "Description of Minnesota." *Collections of the Minnesota Historical Society* 1 (1872): 37–42.

———. "Memoir of Jean Baptiste Faribault." *Collections of the Minnesota Historical Society* 3 (1880): 168–77.

———. "Reminiscences: Historical and Personal." *Collections of the Minnesota Historical Society* 1 (1872): 457–85.

Snelling, Henry Hunt. *Memoirs of a Boyhood at Fort Snelling.* Edited by Lewis Beeson. Minneapolis, MN: Privately printed, 1939.

Sneve, Virginia Driving Hawk. *Completing the Circle.* Lincoln: University of Nebraska Press, 1995.

Statutes of the Territory of Wisconsin. Albany, NY: Packard, Van Benthuyson & Co., 1839.

Steckle, Joseph E. *Topographical Sketch of Fort St. Anthony.* 1823. Facsimile, St. Paul: Minnesota Historical Society Press, 1997.

Sterling, Dorothy, ed. *We Are Your Sisters: Black Women in the Nineteenth Century.* 1984. Reprint, New York: W. W. Norton, 1997.

"Stoner's Memories: Story of Early Madison Told by One Who Arrived in 1837." *Madison Journal,* June 6–7, 1896.

Taliaferro, Lawrence. "The Autobiography of Maj. Lawrence Taliaferro." *Minnesota Historical Collections* 6 (1894): 189–256.

"The Territorial Census for 1836." *Collections of the State Historical Society of Wisconsin* 13 (1895): 247–70.

Thorpe, Francis Newton, ed. *The Federal and State Constitutions, Colonial Charters, and Other Organic Laws of the State, Territories, and Colonies Now Heretofore Forming the United States of America.* 7 volumes. Washington DC: Government Printing Office, 1909.

Thwaites, Reuben Gold. "Narrative of Morgan L. Martin, in an Interview with the Editor." *Collections of the State Historical Society of Wisconsin* 11 (1888): 385–415.

———. "Sketch of Morgan L. Martin." *Collections of the State Historical Society of Wisconsin* 11 (1888): 380–84.

———. "The Territorial Census for 1836." *Wisconsin Historical Collections* 13 (1895): 247–70.

U.S. Congress. *An Act Establishing the Territorial Government of Wisconsin, Statutes at Large.* 5, 15, 1836.

U.S. Congress. *Annals of Congress.* House of Representatives, 15th Cong., 2nd sess., 305–10.

U.S. Congress. *House Journal.* 15th Cong., 2nd Sess., February 16, 1819.

Van Cleve, Charlotte Ouisconsin. *Memories of Fort Snelling and Other Parts of the West.* 1888. Reprint, Philadelphia, PA: Pavilion Press, 2004.

Warren, William E. *History of the Ojibway People.* 1885. Reprint, St. Paul: Minnesota Historical Society Press, 1984.

Williamson, T. S. "Who Were the First Men?" *Collections of the Minnesota State Historical Society* 1 (1872): 295–301.

Wilson, Waziyatawin Angela. *Remember This!: Dakota Decolonization and the Eli Taylor Narratives.* Translated by Wahpetunwin Carolynn Schommer. Lincoln: University of Nebraska Press, 2005.

Zemen, Carrie Reber, and Kathryn Zabelle Derounian-Stodola, eds. *A Thrilling Narrative of Indian Captivity: Dispatches from the Dakota War.* Lincoln: University of Nebraska Press, 2012.

SECONDARY SOURCES

Allen, Felicity. *Jefferson Davis: Unconquerable Heart.* Columbia: University of Missouri Press, 1999.

Anderson, Gary Clayton. *Kinsmen of Another Kind: Dakota-White Relations in the Upper Mississippi Valley, 1650–1862.* St. Paul: Minnesota Historical Society Press, 1997.

Baker, Van R., ed. *The Websters: Letters of an American Army Family in Peace and War, 1836–1853.* Kent, OH: Kent State University Press, 2000.

Bardaglio, Peter W. *Reconstructing the Household: Families, Sex, and the Law in the Nineteenth-Century South.* Chapel Hill: University of North Carolina Press, 1995.

Basso, Keith. *Wisdom Sits in Places: Landscape and Language Among the Western Apache.* Albuquerque: University of New Mexico Press, 1996, 2001.

Belmessous, Saliha, ed. *Native Claims: Indigenous Law against Empire, 1500–1920.* Oxford: Oxford University Press, 2012.

Berkhofer, Robert F., Jr. *The White Man's Indian: Images of the American Indian from Columbus to the Present Day.* New York: Vintage Books, 1979.

Berkin, Carol. *A Brilliant Solution: Inventing the American Constitution.* Orlando, FL: Harvest/Harcourt Inc., 2003.

Brown, Jennifer S. H. *Strangers in Blood: Fur Trade Families in Indian Country.* Norman: University of Oklahoma Press, 1980.

Bynum, Victoria E. *Unruly Women: The Politics of Social and Sexual Control in the Old South.* Chapel Hill: University of North Carolina Press, 1992.

Callender, John M. *New Light on Old Fort Snelling: An Archaeological Exploration, 1957–58.* St. Paul: Minnesota Historical Society, 1959.

Carroll, Jane Lamm. "'This Higgledy Piggledy Assembly': The McLeods, an Anglo-Dakota Family in Early Minnesota." *Minnesota History* 60:6 (Summer 2007): 218–33.

———. "'Who was Jane Lamott?': Anglo-Dakota Daughters in Early Minnesota." *Minnesota History* 59:5 (Spring 2005): 184–96.

Cleary, Catherine B. "Married Women's Property Rights in Wisconsin, 1846–1872." *Wisconsin Magazine of History* 78.12 (Winter 1994–95): 110–37.

Cohen, Felix. *Handbook of Federal Indian Law.* 1942. Revised edition, Charlottesville: Miche, Bobbs-Merrill, 1982.

Cott, Nancy F. "Divorce and the Changing Status of Women in Eighteenth-Century Massachusetts." *William and Mary Quarterly* 33 (October 1976): 586–614.

———. *Public Vows: A History of Marriage and Nation.* Cambridge, MA: Harvard University Press, 2000.

Cruikshank, Ernest Alexander. "Robert Dickson, the Indian Trader." *Collections of the State Historical Society of Wisconsin* 12 (1892): 133–53.

Dewdney, Selwyn. *The Sacred Scrolls of the Southern Ojibway.* Toronto: University of Toronto Press, 1975.

Dictionary of Wisconsin History. http://www.wisconsinhistory.org/dictionary/.

Durand, Paul. *Where the Waters Gather and the Rivers Meet: An Atlas of the Eastern Sioux.* Edited by Robin Siev Durand. Faribault, MN: Paul C. Durand, 1994.

Ekberg, Carl J. *Stealing Indian Women: Native Slavery in the Illinois Country.* Urbana: University of Illinois Press, 2007.

Fehrenbacher, Don E. *Sectional Crisis and Southern Constitutionalism.* Baton Rouge: Louisiana State University Press, 1995.

Feller, Daniel. *The Jacksonian Promise: America, 1815–1840.* Baltimore, MD: Johns Hopkins University Press, 1995.

Finkelman, Paul. "The Northwest Ordinance: A Constitution for an Empire of Liberty." In *Pathways to the Old Northwest: An Observance of the Bicentennial of the Northwest Ordinance,* edited by Andrew Robert Lee Cayton. Indianapolis: Indiana Historical Society, 1988.

Fletcher, Williams J. "Memoir of Captain Martin Scott." *Collections of the Minnesota Historical Society* 3 (1880): 180–87.

Gelles, Edith Belle. "Abigail Adams: Domesticity and the American Revolution." *The New England Quarterly* 52.4 (December 1979): 500–521.

———. *Abigail Adams: A Writing Life.* New York: Routledge, 2002.

———. "Bonds of Friendship: The Correspondence of Abigail Adams and Mercy Otis Warren." *Proceedings of the Massachusetts Historical Society.* 3rd Series, Vol. 108 (1996): 35–71.

Gibbon, Guy. *The Sioux: The Dakota and Lakota Nations.* Malden, MA: Blackwell Publishing, 2003.

Gilman, Rhoda R. *Henry Hastings Sibley: Divided Heart.* St. Paul: Minnesota Historical Society Press, 2004.

———. "How Henry Sibley Took the Road to New Hope." *Minnesota History* 52.6 (Summer 1991): 220–29.

Goodman, Nancy, and Robert Goodman. *Joseph R. Brown: Adventurer on the Minnesota Frontier, 1820–1849.* Rochester, MN: Lone Oak Press, 1996.

Grossberg, Michael. *Governing the Hearth: Law and the Family in Nineteenth Century America.* Chapel Hill: University of North Carolina Press, 1985.

Hamilton, Holman. "Zachary Taylor and Minnesota." *Minnesota History* 30.2 (June 1949): 97–110.

Hansen, Marcus. *Old Fort Snelling, 1819–1858.* Minneapolis, MN: Ross and Haines, Inc., 1958.

Hartog, Hendrik. *Husband and Wife in America: A History.* Cambridge, MA: Harvard University Press, 2000.

Hatheway, Franklin. "Surveying in Wisconsin in 1837." *Wisconsin Historical Collections* 15 (1900): 390–99.

Hilger, M. Inez. *Chippewa Child Life and Its Cultural Background.* 1951. Reprint with introduction by Jean M. O'Brien, St. Paul: Minnesota Historical Society Press, 1992.

Hollon, W. Eugene. *The Lost Pathfinder: Zebulon Montgomery Pike.* Norman: University of Oklahoma Press, 1949.

Holmes, Jerry. *Thomas Jefferson: A Chronology of His Thoughts.* Lanham, MD: Rowman & Littlefield, 2002.

Holton, Woody. *Abigail Adams.* New York: Free Press, 2010.

———. *Unruly Americans and the Origins of the Constitution.* New York: Hill and Wang, 2007.

Horton, James Oliver. *Free People of Color: Inside the African American Community.* Washington, DC: Smithsonian Institution Press, 1993.

Horton, James, and Lois E. Horton. *In Hope of Liberty: Culture, Community and Protest Among Northern Free Blacks, 1700–1860.* New York: Oxford University Press, 1997.

Hotopp, John A., et al. *A Cultural Resource Assessment of the Proposed Reroute for Trunk Highway 55, 54th Street to County Road 62: Hennepin County, Minnesota.* Prepared for the U.S. Department of Transportation, Federal Highway Administration, and the Minnesota Department of Transportation, St. Paul, Minnesota. Marion, IA: Cultural Resource Group, Louis Berger & Associates, 1999.

Hoxie, Frederick E., Ronald Hoffman, and Peter J. Albert, eds. *Native Americans and the Early Republic.* Charlottesville: University Press of Virginia, 1999.

Huston, James L. *Calculating the Value of the Union: Slavery, Property Rights, and the Economic Origins of the Civil War.* Chapel Hill: University of North Carolina Press, 2003.

Hyman, Colette A. *Dakota Women's Work: Creativity, Culture, and Exile.* St. Paul: Minnesota Historical Society Press, 2012.

Johns, Verlan R., Katherine C. Johns, Susan Queripel, and Ted Lofstrom. "An Early Nineteenth Century Occupation of Pike Island, Dakota County, Minnesota." *Minnesota Archaeologist* 36.2 (July 1977): 50–60.

Johnson, Richard W. "Fort Snelling from Its Foundation to the Present Time." *Collections of the Minnesota Historical Society* 8 (1898): 427–48.

Jones, Evan. *Citadel in the Wilderness: The Story of Fort Snelling and the Northwest Frontier.* 1966. Reprint, Minneapolis: University of Minnesota Press, 2001.

Jung, Patrick J. "Judge James Duane Doty and Wisconsin's First Court: The Additional Court of Michigan Territory, 1823–1836." *Wisconsin Magazine of History* 86.2 (Winter 2002–03): 32–41.

Kann, Mark E. *A Republic of Men: The American Founders, Gendered Language, and Patriarchal Politics.* New York: New York University Press, 1998.

Kaplan, Anne R., and Marilyn Ziebarth, eds. *Making Minnesota Territory, 1849–1858.* St. Paul: Minnesota Historical Society Press, 1999.

Kerber, Linda K. *No Constitutional Right to be Ladies: Women and the Obligations of Citizenship.* New York: Hill and Wang, 1998.

———. *Women of the Republic: Intellect and Ideology in Revolutionary America.* Chapel Hill: University of North Carolina Press, 1980.

Kugel, Rebecca. *To Be the Main Leaders of Our People: A History of Minnesota Ojibwe Politics, 1825–1898.* East Lansing: Michigan State University Press, 1998.

Leavenworth, Elias Worther, and William Leavenworth. *A Genealogy of the Leavenworth Family in the United States.* Syracuse, NY: S. G. Hitchcock and Co., 1873.

Lebsock, Suzanne. *The Free Women of Petersburg: Status and Culture in a Southern Town, 1784–1860.* New York: Norton, 1985.

Lewis, James E., Jr. *John Quincy Adams: Policymaker for the Union.* Wilmington, DE: Scholarly Resources, 2001.

Luecke, Barbara K. *Feeding the Frontier Army, 1775–1865.* 1990. Reprint, St. Paul, MN: Grenadier Publications, 2011.

McCurdy, John Gilbert. *Citizen Bachelors: Manhood and the Creation of the United States.* Ithaca, NY: Cornell University Press, 2009.

McCurry, Stephanie. *Masters of Small Worlds: Yeoman Households, Gender Relations, and the Political Cultures of the Antebellum South.* New York: Oxford University Press, 1995.

Meron, Theodor. "The Authority to Make Treaties in the Late Middle Ages." *American Journal of International Law* 89.1 (January 1995): 1–20.

Morice, R. P. A.-G., *Dictionaire Historique des Canadiens et Métis Français de L'Ouest.* Quebec: J. P. Garneau, 1908.

Morrison, Michael. *Slavery and the American West: The Eclipse of Manifest Destiny and the Coming of the Civil War.* Chapel Hill: University of North Carolina Press, 1997.

Murphy, Lucy Eldersveld. *A Gathering of Rivers: Indians, Métis and Mining in the Western Great Lakes, 1737–1832.* Lincoln: University of Nebraska Press, 2000.

Nash, Gary. *The Unknown American Revolution: The Unruly Birth of Democracy and the Struggle to Create America.* New York: Viking, 2005.

Obst, Janis. "Abigail Snelling: Military Wife, Military Widow." *Minnesota History* 54.3 (Fall 1994): 98–111.

Ostler, Jeffrey. *The Plains Sioux and U.S. Colonialism from Lewis and Clark to Wounded Knee.* New York: Cambridge University Press, 2004.

Parker, Henry S. "Henry Leavenworth: Pioneer General." *Military Review* 50.12 (1970): 58–61.

Parsons, Lynn Hudson. *John Quincy Adams.* Madison, WI: Madison House, 1998.

Pascoe, Peggy. *What Comes Naturally: Miscegenation Law and the Making of Race in America.* New York: Oxford University Press, 2009.

Pateman, Carole. *The Sexual Contract.* Stanford, CA: Stanford University Press, 1988.

Prucha, Francis Paul. *American Indian Policy in the Formative Years: The Indian Trade and Intercourse Acts, 1790–1834.* Cambridge, MA: Harvard University Press, 1962.

———. *Broadax and Bayonet: The Role of the United States Army in the Development of the Northwest, 1815–1860.* Madison: State Historical Society of Wisconsin, 1953.

Purdue, Theda, and Michael D. Green, eds. *The Cherokee Removal: A Brief History with Documents.* Boston: Bedford Books, 1995.

Rentmeester, Les, and Jeanne Rentmeester. *The Wisconsin Creoles.* Melbourne, FL: Privately published, 1987.

Riley, Glenda. *Divorce: An American Tradition.* New York: Oxford University Press, 1991.

Saler, Bethel. "Negotiating the Treaty Polity: Gender, Race, and the Transformation of Wisconsin from Indian Country into an American State, 1776–1854." PhD diss., University of Wisconsin–Madison, 1999.

Salmon, Marilynn. *Women and the Law of Property in Early America.* Chapel Hill: University of North Carolina Press, 1986.

Samples, John, ed. *James Madison and the Future of Limited Government.* Washington, DC: Cato Institute, 2002.

Satz, Ronald N. *Chippewa Treaty Rights: The Reserved Rights of Wisconsin's Chippewa Indians in Historical Perspective.* Madison: Wisconsin Academy of Sciences, Arts and Letters, 1991.

Schenck, Theresa M. *"The Voice of the Crane Echoes Far": The Sociopolitical Organization of the Lake Superior Ojibwa, 1640–1855.* New York: Garland Publishing, Inc., 1997.

Schwalm, Leslie A. *'A Hard Fight for We': Women's Transition from Slavery to Freedom in Lowcountry South Carolina.* Urbana: University of Illinois Press, 1997.

———. "'Overrun with Free Negroes': Emancipation and Wartime Migration in the Upper Midwest." *Civil War History* 50 (2004): 145–74.

Schwartzenback, Sibyl A., and Patricia Smith, eds. *Women and the United States Constitution: History, Interpretation, and Practice.* New York: Columbia University Press, 2003.

Seale, Mark, and Kenneth W. Stevenson, eds. *Documents of the Marriage Liturgy.* Collegeville, MN: Liturgical Press, 1992.

Shammas, Carole. *A History of Household Government in America.* Charlottesville: University of Virginia Press, 2002.

Skinner, Claiborne A. *The Upper Country: French Enterprise in the Colonial Great Lakes.* Baltimore, MD: Johns Hopkins University Press, 2008.

Sleeper-Smith, Susan. *Indian Women and French Men: Rethinking Cultural Encounter in the Western Great Lakes.* Amherst: University of Massachusetts Press, 2001.

Smith, Barbara Clark. *The Freedoms We Lost: Consent and Resistance in Revolutionary America.* New York: The New Press, 2010.

Smith, Daniel Scott. "The Demographic History of Colonial New England." *The Journal of Economic History* 32.1 (March 1972): 165–83.

———. "Female Householding in Late Eighteenth-Century America and the Problem of Poverty." *Journal of Social History* 28.1 (Fall 1994): 83–107.

Spector, Janet D. *What This Awl Means: Feminist Archaeology at a Wahpeton Dakota Village.* St. Paul: Minnesota Historical Society Press, 1993.

Sterling, Dorothy, ed. *We Are Your Sisters: Black Women in the Nineteenth Century.* 1984. Reprint, New York: W. W. Norton, 1997.

Treuer, Anton. *Living Our Language: Ojibwe Tales and Oral Histories.* St. Paul: Minnesota Historical Society Press, 2001.

Treuer, David. *Rez Life: An Indian's Journey Through Reservation Life.* New York: Atlantic Monthly Press, 2012.

Van Kirk, Sylvia. *Many Tender Ties: Women in Fur-Trade Society, 1670–1870.* Norman: University of Oklahoma Press, 1980.

VanderVelde, Lea. *Mrs. Dred Scott: A Life on Slavery's Frontier.* Oxford: Oxford University Press, 2009.

VanderVelde, Lea, and Sandhya Subramanian. "Mrs. Dred Scott." *Yale Law Journal* 106.4 (January 1997): 1033–1120.

Wallace, Anthony F. C. *The Long Bitter Trail: Andrew Jackson and the Indians.* New York: Hill and Wang, 1993.

Waziyatawin. *What Does Justice Look Like?: The Struggle for Liberation in Dakota Homeland.* St. Paul: Living Justice Press, 2008.

White, Helen McCann. *Guide to a Microfilm Edition of the Lawrence Taliaferro Papers.* St. Paul: Minnesota Historical Society, 1966.

White, Helen, and Bruce White. *Fort Snelling in 1838: An Ethnographic and Historical Study.* St. Paul: Turnstone Historical Research, 1998.

White, Richard. *The Middle Ground: Indians, Empires, and Republics in the Great Lakes Region, 1610–1815.* New York: Cambridge University Press, 1991.

Wingerd, Mary Lethert. *North Country: The Making of Minnesota.* Minneapolis: University of Minnesota Press, 2010.

Wisconsin Cartographer's Guild. *Wisconsin's Past and Present: A Historical Atlas.* Madison: University of Wisconsin Press, 1998.

Zagarri, Rosemarie. *Revolutionary Backlash: Women and Politics in the Early American Republic.* Philadelphia: University of Pennsylvania Press, 2007.

Zeman, Carrie Rebe, and Kathryn Zabelle Derounian-Stodola, eds. *A Thrilling Narrative of Indian Captivity: Dispatches from the Dakota War.* Lincoln: University of Nebraska Press, 2012.

Index

Printed in the USA
CPSIA information can be obtained
at www.ICGtesting.com
JSHW082206140824
68134JS00014B/452